UP THE LAKE WITH A PADDLE

CANOE AND KAYAK GUIDE

VOLUME I

Sierra Foothills and Sacramento Region

BY WILLIAM VAN DER VEN

Fine Edge Productions

IMPORTANT LEGAL NOTICE AND DISCLAIMER

Outdoor activities are an assumed risk sport. This book cannot take the place of appropriate instruction for paddling, swimming, or lifesaving techniques. Bodies of water by nature contain hazards and they change with time and conditions. Every effort has been made to make this guide as accurate as possible, but it is the ultimate responsibility of the paddler to judge his or her ability and act accordingly.

The editors, author, publishers, and distributors accept no liability for any errors or omissions in this book or for any injuries or losses incurred from using this book.

Credits

Cover Photo: William Van der Ven
Author Photo: Rhoda Mantell
Photographs within text: William Van der Ven
Book design, maps and illustrations by Faith Ann Rumm
and Melanie Haage Design
Edited by Réanne Hemingway-Douglass

LIBRARY OF CONGRESS CATALOGING-ON-PUBLICATION DATA

Van der Ven, William, 1949—
    Up the lake with a paddle : canoe and kayak guide / by William Van der Ven. — 1st ed.
        p.   cm.
    Contents: v.   1.   Sierra Foothills and Sacramento Region
    ISBN 0-938665-54-5 (v. 1)
    1.   Canoes and canoeing—California, Northern—Guidebooks.
2.   Kayaking—California, Northern—Guidebooks.   3.   California, Northern—Guidebooks.   I.   Title.
GV776.C2V36 1998   98-16844
917.94—dc21   CIP

ISBN 0-938665-54-5
Copyright © 1998 by Fine Edge Productions

Address requests for permission to:
Fine Edge Productions, Route 2, Box 303, Bishop, CA 93514
www.fineedge.com
Printed in the United States of America
First Edition

CONTENTS

Acknowledgments

I wish to thank many people whose help and support kept me on my goal. First of all, Dan Conner who, after a long evening of drinking French Roast <u>and</u> Pepsi, came up with the title for this book.

Lisa Ross, whose enthusiastic support and constant belief in the need for this book helped me overcome my doubts. Also, many thanks to Lisa's son Alexander J. F. "Sandy" Ross, for the painstaking task of proofreading and including many thoughtful suggestions. However, any errors and mistakes in the text are all mine!

John, Kirk, Ann, Urs, Spencer, JT, Adam, and the rest of the wonderful folks with whom I work with at CCK: their continued interest in the outcome of this project helped me pound those keys when I'd rather have been boating.

To Deborah Valturno, master kayaker, for all the tips and advice. May it always be a "Coaster!"

Kurt Renner of We No Nah Canoes & Current Design Kayaks and John Seals of Dagger Canoes & Stohlquist Water Ware whose support is always appreciated.

Mr. Bill Griffith, septuagenarian and the dean of canoeing in Sacramento, multiple winner of *Eppies Great Race,* for his help; especially for teaching me the proper way to tie an "Artillery Knot" . . . and the rest of the ropes.

Sheri, owner of Barnstormer Books, whose knowledge of books, cheerful assistance and competitive prices, has allowed me to build a first class reference library.

I am deeply grateful to my wife for understanding my need to "put my paddle where my mouth is" and finish the book. Without her assistance and computer literacy, this book would never have materialized.

Finally, to my son Peter: thank you for not laughing on that day in the slough!

Introduction

"Hi. I'm new here and looking for a place to paddle. Nothing rough, no difficult white water. You know, some type of quiet water where I can take my family or a friend. Anybody know of a place nearby?"

In the eight years that I've been in the paddle sport business, many people have asked me to suggest places of the quiet kind to paddle rather than those that are technically difficult. Little written material was available; now *Up the Lake with a Paddle* fills that gap.

The beautiful rivers, lakes, cascading whitewater, and tidal rhythms of the Delta offer boaters an exceptional variety of paddling opportunities in the Sierra foothills and greater Sacramento area. I have paddled every lake and river described in this guidebook and my experience and personal knowledge, aided by detailed research, insures the reader in-depth information.

What's more, *Up the Lake with a Paddle* specifically addresses the

Smooth paddling

questions of the canoeist or touring kayaker such as: Is there a fee for cars carrying boats? How far is the put-in/take-out from the parking area? If there is a portage, how long is it and what is the terrain? Which direction does the wind blow, how strong is it? Are there rocks, snags, current, rapids or other hazards? Are there beaches suitable for landing?

In deciding whether or not to include a particular paddle trip, I looked at the following considerations:

1. *Driving time and accessibility:* Is the location more than two to four hours driving distance from Sacramento? If a shuttle is necessary, how long is it? What are the conditions of the access roads? How accessible are the landings?

2. *Paddle difficulty:* Does it meet the definition of quiet water? How many miles is the paddle? Is it suitable for a novice paddler or family outing or is a higher skill level necessary to insure safety? Are there portages? Hazards? Can wind or tide become a factor?

3. *Would I want to return?* Is there more to explore? Are there nearby hikes or walks? If I want to stay overnight, what are the conditions of the campsites?

With this guidebook in hand, you'll have all the information you need for a fun-filled and safe excursion. *"May the wind be on your back and the warmth of the sun on your shoulders. Happy Paddling!"*

Definition of Moving Water

Just what is "quiet water" boating and how do we gauge white water paddling? Quiet water, flat water, and sometimes even non-moving water all have one thing in common: they are bodies of water that have little or no current. The main source of surface activity comes from wind gusts or is man-made.

There are two primary characteristics of moving water that determine how challenging a boating experience could become. The first is the gradient of a river; the second is the flow of water.

Gradient refers to how a river drops or descends along its bed per river mile. The flow of a river pertains to the continuous output or water volume in an average year. This mass of water is measured in cubic feet per second (CFS). An example would be the middle fork of the American River; the gradient is 22 feet per mile, but the flow is averaged at 1100 CFS.

Although gradient and flow determine the level of challenge to paddling a given river, certain sections of the same river may be classified at different levels of expertise. Boaters rate rivers according to the difficulty of rapids to be run. The six categories of difficulty based on normal flow are:

Class I: EASY Barely moving water with a few riffles, small waves and no obstacles.

Class II: MEDIUM Rapids have bigger waves but no major obstructions in the channel.

Class III: DIFFICULT Rapids become technical because route-finding is sometimes necessary. The rapids become bigger and longer than Class II rapids. Deep holes, large standing waves and hidden pour-overs require scouting before running by less experienced boaters.

Class IV: VERY DIFFICULT Strong, powerful rapids containing deep holes with churning eddies that require precise route-finding and a solid knowledge of boat-handling skills. Scouting is necessary and portaging around the rapid are prudent.

Class V: EXTREMELY DIFFICULT These are very long and violent rapids with large wave trains, huge holes, and boiling eddies. The rapids are run only by very experienced boaters, usually in white water kayaks or canoes.

Class VI: LIMIT OF NAVIGABILITY These rapids are to be considered dangerous and at the limit of a boater's ability to run and survive. A thorough knowledge of boating and paddling skills under controlled conditions is a necessity before attempting to negotiate these rapids.

Finally, it is important to remember that these ratings are to be increased when the areas to be paddled are located in remote areas. (After Cassady, J., Cross, B., Calhoun, F. in *Western White Water*, p. 4; Jacobson, C. in *Canoeing Wild Rivers*, Appendix E.)

In addition to the rapids, the flows of the majority of rivers in California are dam-controlled. What I mean is that discharges from a dam, either for hydroelectric purposes or for flood control, determine the time and extent of the flow. This factor has necessitated the daily ritual of phoning ahead for flow times and release rates.

Needless to say, this rating system applies only to moving water (i.e. white water boating) and not to any lake or reservoir. This does not mean that paddling on a lake or any quiet water is risk free.

Different hazards exist that must be taken into account for a safe and enjoyable boating experience. Paddlers should be familiar with their gear, wear appropriate life jackets, and know the extent of their limitations.

The primary hazard of open water boating, such as on lakes, bays and reservoirs, is the wind. The direction of the wind can make or break a paddler's day. Paddling into a continuous headwind blowing ten to fifteen miles per hour on the return leg of a lake paddle can become physically grueling and mentally draining when the added worry of capsizing is prevalent.

In my choice of paddling locations, I have attempted to describe only those rivers whose classification of difficulty rate I or II on the scale of I through VI. For the lakes and reservoirs, I include a description of wind and weather conditions, and other obstacles I encountered when paddling there.

Using This Guide

Each paddle description is divided into five major parts:

Trip Length: Generally given in miles, either one way or round trip.

Maps: U.S. Geological Survey topographical sections and, where appropriate, a gazetteer or atlas.

Access: Given in miles, with Sacramento as the originating reference point.

Difficulty of the Paddle: Description of the conditions or hazards encountered, such as gusting winds, submerged rocks, strong currents, or other less-obvious dangers.

Trip Description: Highlights of an area, as well as some historical background and natural history. Additional detailed information is described in the sidebars **"In the Eddy."**

Other Sources: Maps, guidebooks and periodicals of interest appear at the end of each chapter.

Readers interested in more details about areas described should consult the bibliography.

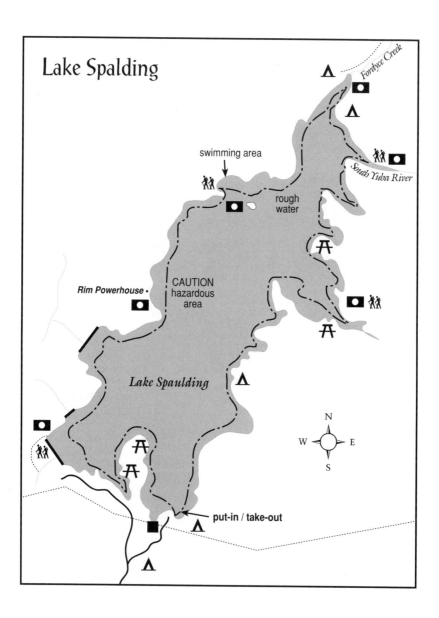

Lake Spalding

Fordyce Creek

swimming area

rough water

South Yuba River

CAUTION hazardous area

Rim Powerhouse

Lake Spaulding

N
W   E
S

put-in / take-out

CHAPTER 1

High Sierra Paddling Areas

Paddling Area 1: Lake Spalding

Trip Length: The lake, which cover 698 acres, can be paddled in one day. If you include hiking the back country around Fordyce Creek and the South Yuba River, plan on a minimum of two days.

Maps: **USGS Topographic Quadrants:**
Blue Canyon, CA., 7.5 minute series
Cisco Grove, CA., 7.5 minute series

Northern California Atlas and Gazetteer, Delorme Mapping Co., 1988, grid #80

Access: From Sacramento, take I-80 East past Yuba Gap and exit on State Highway 20 West. Pay attention to the exit speed because the turn is extremely abrupt. Continue on Highway 20 for approximately 2 miles. Turn right onto Lake Spaulding Road approximately 100 feet past the brown Lake Spaulding Recreation Area sign. Drive past the PG & E employee housing area, through the campground

Lake Spaulding

entrance gate, then follow the signs to the parking area. (*Note*: Drive with caution. The narrow paved road leading to the lake from the campground is a two-lane road built for one-way traffic.) If the parking area is empty, park next to the restroom adjacent to the boat ramp entrance. This will give you a short walk to the water with your boat. If you must use the boat launch, be prepared to pay a launch fee ($5 in 1997). Otherwise, there is no charge for carrying and hand-launching cartop boats.

If you are planning to stay overnight, the walk-in campground is on the right as you drove in, next to the camp host's site. Those of you who are boat camping can expect to pay $5 per vehicle per night for parking. If the camp host is not available, obtain a pay envelope from the information sign adjacent to the campground entrance and deposit the amount into the "iron ranger" (that green metal pipe stuck in the ground). No cash? No problem! Write a check for the amount made out to R.F.M.

Difficulty: **For a small Sierra lake, Lake Spaulding gets a lot of use. Because of the lake's popularity, everyone from wind surfers to water skiers use this lake. As a paddler, be prepared for speeding motor craft in all shapes and sizes and the cross wakes they cause.** Although the prevailing wind is from the west, I have encountered shifting headwinds paddling from one end of the lake to the other. The lake also produces what is sometimes known as a "blow." From a dead calm, a wind will suddenly arise strong enough to create whitecaps. Similarly, just as quickly, the wind dies out.

Please heed the warning signs around the powerhouse. Sudden surges of water may be released with little or no warning. This also pertains to the mouth of the small stream located just past the northeast end of the powerhouse. For a visual impression of the amount of discharge that may occur, check out the photograph on the bulletin board next to the "iron ranger."

As the water level drops in the summer, keep an eye out for barely submerged granite outcrops. This hazard is more prevalent on the upper part of the lake.

Tom Steinstra, in his guidebook on California boating (*California Boating and Water Sports*, p. 223), aptly describes Lake Spaulding as a lake whose surroundings were chiseled into being. This chiseled look was created in part through the work of ice when glaciers dominated the scenery in the Sierra.

Glacial polish is abundant in this area.

If this is your first time on Lake Spaulding, I would suggest that you paddle the lake in a clockwise direction. Upon launching, head toward the point on your left, in the direction of the dam. If you started early, the sun will light the western shore and provide you with a bright, scenic photo opportunity. As you round the first point, follow the shoreline and you will enter a small cove where there are a couple of nice beaches to take a break.

If you follow the first cove around, look at the northwestern end for a granite wall from which the sun reflects off the sides like small mirrors; this is a good example of glacial polish. You will be able to spot many such examples throughout the rocks surrounding the lake. As you come around the southwest end of the cove, notice the mossy top of a snag jutting out of the lake.

The main dam visible from I-80 as you come over the crest at Emigrant Gap is now in front of you. A small wooden structure on top of the dam adds a nice touch to any photograph taken of the dam. There are two other dams that hold back the waters to make the lake.

Eventually you paddle around a point after passing the small bay containing the third concrete dam. If the lighting is right, you will catch a pretty view of the powerhouse and the discharge of water used for the generation of hydroelectric power. Again, please heed the warnings and do not go past the buoy markers.

The next place of interest is the inlet to the creek adjacent to the powerhouse. *Do not linger here admiring the small waterfall;* unexpected discharges may cause the level of the stream to rise and create heavy turbulence.

Inlet to Lake Spaulding

Take time to admire the granite outcrops that seem to slide out of the lake. Small bands of lighter rock that streak through this parent rock or zigzag in various directions are veins of quartz or quartzite, created when the granite magma was cooling. For a more informative description, read Mary Hill's gem of a book *Geology of the Sierra Nevada,* pp. 64-68.

When I paddled the lake in early summer, bands of pale swallowtail butterflies with their black and white markings flitted around my boat. Some even landed on the colored deck bag on the foredeck of my kayak.

Since the extensive flooding in 1997, massive piles of driftwood have covered the beaches and shoreline. Some of the shapes and sizes would make an interesting natural sculpture.

Just before you reach a small island, you pass a rocky point that acts as a wind break to a lovely sandy beach. If the weather is nice, pull in and take a swim in the clear water. If you have time, hike to the first small granite dome sitting below Zion Hill. From up there you have a great view of the lake and upper Bear Valley below the dam.

The paddle to the small island from the point should be short and sweet. Make your approach and landing just behind the small band of cottonwoods on the western end of the island. The island appears to be the top of a drowned granite dome. Looking at the granite surface, notice the smooth polish, the result of a glacier grinding its way across the rock. As you start hiking to the top of the dome, look for small but deep grooves running across the surface of the granite, striations that were formed by stones carried along with the movements of the glacier. The large boulders lying around the surface of the dome may be "**erratics**," a name given to those rocks or boulders left behind by retreating glaciers.

Where the rock has weathered and built up a soil base, small bunches of vegetation have taken root. The predominate shrub is manzanita. Where the rock has broken down and allowed soil and moisture to accumulate, clusters of wildflowers begin to grow. I have spotted alpine paintbrush and sulfur flowers throughout the area of the dome. On a last note, some of the rock appears to be "peeling," as on the skin of an onion. This erosional process, known as **exfoliation**, is characteristic of Sierra granites. As the rock weathers, it produces the distinctive dome shape seen throughout the Sierra.

If you paddle toward the northern point and entrance to the narrow inlet that used to be a valley of Fordyce Creek, be prepared for sudden wind gusts that generate strong breaking wavelets striking on the beam of your boat.

Where Fordyce Creek spills into the lake there is an attractive camp spot. If you are fortunate to arrive and see it empty, grab it quick! In the spring and early summer, before the water level drops, this is a very popular spot. Sometimes if the level of the water is right and the run-off from the creek is not too strong, a fun bow-surfing wave is created. For an additional adventure, you can discover numerous small waterfalls are to be discovered if you take the time to hike up the creek bed.

If the first spot is taken, another camp site with a great view of the lower lake is located at the northeast point of the inlet. Continuing on a easterly track, you will spot the narrow inlet that leads to the waterfalls of the South Yuba River. In the late spring when the current is not too strong, paddle up this gorge for the

A relaxing rest spot

highlight of the trip. As you enter the inlet, be sure to look for the tall snag standing apart on the southeast (right) side. With a pair of binoculars you may spot a parent osprey in the nest. When you reach the end of the inlet, you should be able to view a double set of waterfalls where the South Yuba cascades into the lake.

When you leave the inlet, paddle past the first cove on your left, and into the second smaller U-shaped cove. Beach your boat on a gentle granite slab on the south arm of the cove, and hike up to the top of the dome. From here you have an unsurpassed view of the small islands within the drowned mouth of Gonelson Canyon.

After exploring the cove with its islands, you can see the boat ramp and beach where you initially started from. The paddle back will be into a stiff head wind.

In the Eddy

If you have the time, energy and a sense of
adventure, you will appreciate this destination—the
deep pools above the waterfalls of the South Yuba
River. The short hike (approximately 1 mile)
provides you with a spectacular view of the lake and
the surrounding glaciated valley.

When you reach the pools, their beauty and
remoteness make your effort worthwhile. The water
is warm and deep enough to enjoy a swim and the
beaches are clean with no litter or human footprints
to spoil your adventure.

To reach this location, tie off your boats at a small
niche next to a large free-standing granite slab
approximately 100 yards on the right as you paddle
back from the South Yuba waterfalls. Hike up to the
first level of exposed granite. Using the rapids below
as your reference, hike along the ridge pastthe third
rapid. You will pass a gnarled snag with a U.S.
Forest boundary marker nailed into it; this is a

"bearing tree." Go past the tree and cross over the small stream, aiming for the cleared high ground slightly to your right (east). Just before you reach the exposed granite outcrop, you will pass a metal sign marking the boundary of this section of the Tahoe National Forest.

If you feel lost, remember this is an adventure and hopefully you remembered to bring the Cisco Grove Quad. Look for section 10 on the map. Now find the broken line separating section 10 from section 15. You are approximately on the ridge overlooking the small blue pool just below the broken line of the map.

From the granite outcrop where you are standing, hike slightly past the third or last rapid visible below. Look for a natural break in the rock or "chimney" that allows you to scramble down to the river bed. Once you have reached the sand, turn leftand hike past the grove of pines and you will gaze on the first of several quiet water pools.

Before you leave, please take time to pick up any trash and check for items of clothing so other visitors can enjoy the beauty as you did!

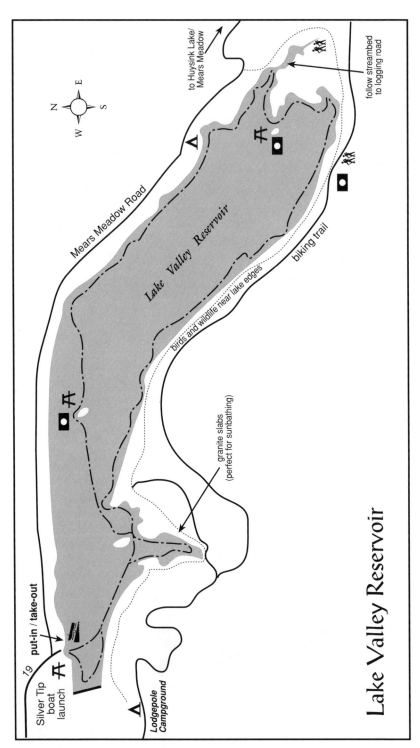

Lake Valley Reservoir

Mears Meadow Road

to Huysink Lake/
Mears Meadow

follow streambed
to logging road

Lake Valley Reservoir

biking trail

birds and wildlife near lake edges

granite slabs
(perfect for sunbathing)

Silver Tip
boat
launch

19 **put-in / take-out**

*Lodgepole
Campground*

N
W   E
S

20

Paddling Area 2: Lake Valley Reservoir

Trip Length: When full, the lake surface covers 300 acres. You can paddle the entire lake in a day. However, if you want to take the time to explore islands and backwaters or hike the surrounding trails, an overnighter is highly recommended.

Maps: USGS Topographic Quadrants:
Cisco Grove, 7.5 minute series

Northern California Atlas & Gazetteer, Delorme Mapping Co., 1988, Section 80, grid B-3

Access: From Sacramento, take Interstate 80 East. Turn off onto the Yuba Gap exit. Follow the road to a Y-intersection with a signboard on a mature Sequoia tree. Make a right onto Lake Valley Rd., and follow it for approximately 1 mile. At the second Y-intersection, make a left onto the dirt road. (**Note:** the paved road continues on to the public campground called Lodgepole Campground operated by PG & E, and a private camp called Sky Mountain. The dirt road is

Forest Road 19, also called Mears Meadow Road.) Proceed to the Silver Tip Picnic Area & Boat Launch located approximately 3/4 mile on the right. This access road into Silver Tip Boat Launch is deeply rutted and contains a few large exposed cobbles. Vehicles with a low clearance should be driven slowly and carefully to the parking area. The boat launch is on the upper right as you drive in. The location is very small with limited parking but it does have a cinder block restroom and a couple of picnic tables overlooking the lake.

Difficulty: Lake Valley Reservoir is an "exposed" lake. By this I mean that there are only a few inlets and islands to block the prevailing west wind. If you paddle to the upper end of the lake, be prepared to battle the wind on your return.

Since water skiing is not allowed, you do not have to watch for speeding boats and the cross wakes they create.

As the water level is drawn down to meet the needs for hydroelectric power, watch for granite outcrops that are barely exposed and difficult to spot.

This is a "full course lake", meaning that when the wind is too strong for paddling, you can take down the mountain bikes and use the old logging roads to explore the back country around the lake. Snorkel or swim in the clear waters at one of the small inlets, or fish for trout in one of the many deep holes around the submerged granite. If you drive or hike a short distance on Forest Road 19, there are some great spots to "boulder" and practice your climbing skills.

So what is there to paddle? The lake has two islands worth exploring and some of the best Sierra scenery this

Paddling in high water

side of Lake Tahoe. When the water level is high, it's fun to paddle among the groves of lichen-covered shaggy sequoias, sunlit aspens and towering lodgepole pine trees that are all standing in high water.

Upon launching your boat, head for the small inlet located across and to the southeast of the lake. The granite wall that you pass on your right, just before the dam, has been sculpted by the work of former glaciers. When the sunlight reaches the wall's surface, small, shiny patches of slick-rock light up like reflections off tiny mirrors. The polished rock was formed when glaciers carrying debris ground down the granite

Sunny rest spot

until it was rubbed smooth and shiny. For a more detailed description of glaciated granite, read the section on Lake Spaulding.

Inside the inlet is a small cove surrounded by granite and conifers. You can spot the small beach area and the smooth slabs of granite that make for comfortable spots to lie and soak in the late afternoon sun. By late afternoon, the water is nice enough to swim in and the rock slabs warm enough to doze on.

Nearby is the lodge that belongs to the Sky Mountain Camp. You will know if it is in use by the shouts and screams of the many kids swimming, canoeing or kayaking near the lodge. As you pass by the lodge you will notice the small rocky island on your left. In front of you is another island—your second destination on this paddle. When you reach the island, the best and only take-out spot is on the northeast side.

In the summer, at least five different species of wildflowers bloom, and I have counted four species of butterflies flitting around the island vegetation. Standing on the exposed granite looking up the lake, the left or northeast shoreline is less forested and has a more gentle slope, creating more beaches to land on. On the negative side, you can hear the sounds of the logging trucks as they shift gears coming down the nearby hill. The southwest side, although not as accessible, contains a greater variety of observable wildlife, particularly different species of birds.

If you are fortunate to be on the lake when it is full, then paddle to the main inlet located on the northeast tip of the lake. Hopefully the entrance to the drainage will be clear and not blocked by fallen timber. If it's clear, enjoy the sensory thrill of a quiet paddle through a light-filled grove of aspen.

Eventually you will reach the cobble bar of the dry streambed where you may beach your boat or turn back. If you have the time, walk up the dry bed until you reach the old logging road. Once you have reached the road (approximately 400 feet from the lake edge), you may hike parallel with the lake and be rewarded with some spectacular views of the lake and surrounding mountains. For further use of this road, read *In the Eddy* at the end of the chapter.

Bring binoculars; the bird watching here is truly outstanding. Because so few people disturb the area, the birds are not wary of your presence. Some of the birds seen in the area include western tanagers, mountain bluebirds, hairy woodpeckers, white-headed woodpeckers, chickadees, nuthatches and of course the loud and boisterous Steller jays.

On your return, stop and beach your boat on the small rocky island off the tip of the tree-covered point. From here you will have a good view of the expanse of the lake. To the northeast is the steep ridge that leads upward toward Cisco Butte. Facing south, you gaze up the graduated slope of McIntosh Hill. The partially forested high ground stretching westward from McIntosh Hill is the area known as Monumental Ridge.

To beat the wind, escape the bright sun, and observe the wildlife of the lake, paddle back along the shaded southwest shoreline. Keep an eye out for deer browsing or resting amongst the low vegetation near the edge of the lake. Small groups of Canada geese and their

young goslings feed on the grasses growing near the stream drainage. On the limbs of the snags standing in the water, you may spot ospreys and belted kingfishers. Chugging along in a straight line of bobbing fuzz is a mother merganser and her brood of chicks.

Eventually the handsome structure of the lodge appears, and then the inlet where the last rays of the sun still warm the water and the surrounding granite create a last-minute opportunity to have a swim and "catch a few rays." From the inlet, you can see the shaded opening where the boat launch is located and your paddle ends.

In the Eddy

When paddling is not possible, try mountain biking. For those of you who like to bike on an established course, visit the Eagle Mountain Bike and Nordic Ski Resort. You'll see the resort on the left upon making the right turn at the first Y-intersection after exiting the freeway.

If you would rather avoid the crowd and spills of the bike course, then try biking the loop trail that circles the lake.

Using the Cisco Grove topographical section map, you can route-plan an enjoyable full day exploring the lake. If you already paddled the inlet described in the section on Lake Valley Reservoir and hiked to the logging road adjacent to the lake, then you know the condition of the road. The road, wide enough for two bikes side by side, is fairly clear of debris and maintains a moderate gradient. Several streams cross the road on the southwest side but no major erosion has taken place.

On the northeast side, pick up Forest Road 19 and use it as a return route. The road becomes a washboard unless it has been recently graded. On weekdays, you will compete with logging trucks for the right-of-way.

If you are really ambitious or want to plan an overnighter, then using your bikes, make the trek to the small but picturesque S P Lakes. Forget the trip to Huysink Lake. It is on private property and the entire lake is posted with "No Trespassing" signs.

Other Sources:

Nevada & Sierra Counties. Compass Maps, 1995 ed.

Guidebooks:

Recreational Lakes of California. Greg Dirksen & Renee Reeves. Burbank, CA. Recreation Sales Publishing, Inc., 1993

California Boating and Watersports. Tom Stienstra. San Francisco, CA. Foghorn Press, 1996

Notes

Great blue heron

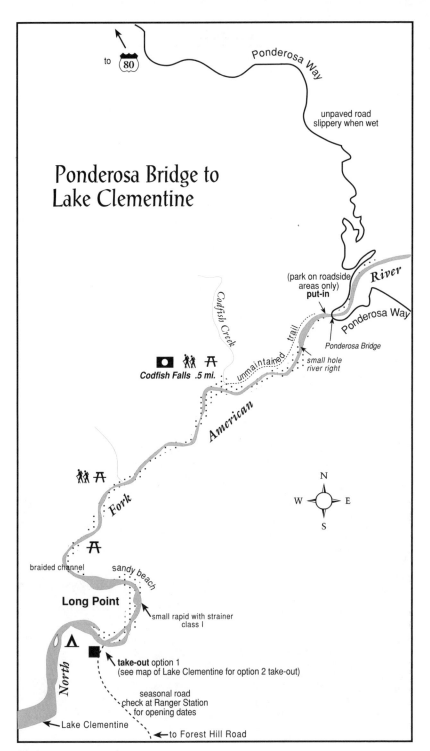

Ponderosa Bridge to Lake Clementine

to [80]

Ponderosa Way

unpaved road
slippery when wet

River

Ponderosa Way

(park on roadside
areas only)
put-in

Ponderosa Bridge

unmaintained trail

*small hole
river right*

Codfish Creek

Codfish Falls .5 mi.

American

Fork

N
W ⊙ E
S

braided channel

sandy beach

Long Point

small rapid with strainer
class I

take-out option 1
(see map of Lake Clementine for option 2 take-out)

seasonal road
check at Ranger Station
for opening dates

North

← Lake Clementine

← to Forest Hill Road

CHAPTER 2

The Sierra Foothills: I-80 Corridor

PADDLING AREA 1:
North Fork of the American River–
Ponderosa Bridge to Lake Clementine

Trip Length: two options
Option 1: 4.3 miles, with the take-out just past Long Point
Option 2: 8.3 miles, with the take-out at Lake Clementine Dam

Maps: **USGS Topographic Quadrants:**
Greenwood, CA., 7.5 minute series
Colfax, CA., 7.5 minute series
Auburn, CA., 7.5 minute series

Access: From Sacramento, take I-80 East to the Weimar exit. Make a right turn onto Ponderosa Way and follow the road to the Ponderosa Bridge crossing the North Fork of the American River. Your put-in will be on the down river (south) side of the bridge. If you don't wish to

North Fork American River

paddle four miles across the lake, choose **Option 1.** This take-out is at the upper end of the lake immediately past the land feature on your map called Long Point. Look for a cobble beach on river left (the left side of the river as you face downstream). Blocked by brush and trees is a campground and a seasonal access road that opens in April. Additional information on fees, the use of this road, camping and overnight parking may be obtained by calling the Auburn State Recreation Area located in Auburn, California (phone 916-885-4527). **Option 2** necessitates paddling the four miles of Lake Clementine and using the boat launch ramp near the marina adjacent to the dam. This location is the most popular and contains a cement boat ramp, wooden dock and parking spaces located above the launching site. See Paddle Area 2 in this chapter for further description.

North Fork Canyon above Long Point

Difficulty: Although this section of the river is considered a class II run, the amount of runoff caused by snow melt and heavy rains creates high water conditions that require solid boat-handling skills. A knowledge of boat/paddler rescue techniques is advisable.

The long shuttle and time-consuming logistics of putting this trip together are offset by the beauty and solitude the paddler will experience on this stretch of river. I have spotted mergansers,

Canada geese, great blue herons, egrets and numerous species of waterfowl feeding on the river banks. One early spring trip, I saw an American bald eagle perching on the limb of a pine tree.

I recommend a very early start for this trip so that paddlers are not caught on the river as the sun sets. However, I also recommend timing your trip with the moon cycle and paddling the lake portion when the moon is full. For a more detailed description of this lake, see the chapter on Lake Clementine.

After the put-in, stay to river left. The first rapid hides a small hole in the center of the drop-off. Be prepared for headwinds when making the left hand bends; when on the lake, the afternoon canyon wind is usually a headwind. I found that by paddling on the lake's west side, the canyons act as a wind break and allow for an easier paddle.

Depending on the flow, the greatest danger to the paddler on this section of the river are the rocks that are obscured by the churning waters. None of the rapids and obstacles are difficult but they do require an intermediary knowledge of paddle strokes and boat-handling proficiency. Due to the remoteness of this stretch of the river, it's prudent to carry a proper first aid kit and have a knowledge of boat rescue and CPR.

Looking up North Fork Canyon

The nearest exit out of the canyon beyond Ponderosa Road is a trail paralleling the river on river right (right side of river as you face downstream). This trail originates at the Ponderosa Bridge and ends at Codfish Creek. No other exit from the river exists until you reach Long Point on river right, approximately four miles from the put-in. At Long Point a dirt road located beyond the cobble beach (in the center of the point) connects to the main road at Clipper Creek.

First bend around Long Point

In the Eddy

Codfish Creek / Codfish Falls: Look for a sand and gravel bar to river right approximately one mile down river. A trail follows the creek up to Codfish Falls one-half mile from the river. If gold panning is your forte, this is a good spot to try your luck. For a view of Codfish Falls, follow the trail upstream for approximately 1/2 mile.

Notes

Lake Clementine

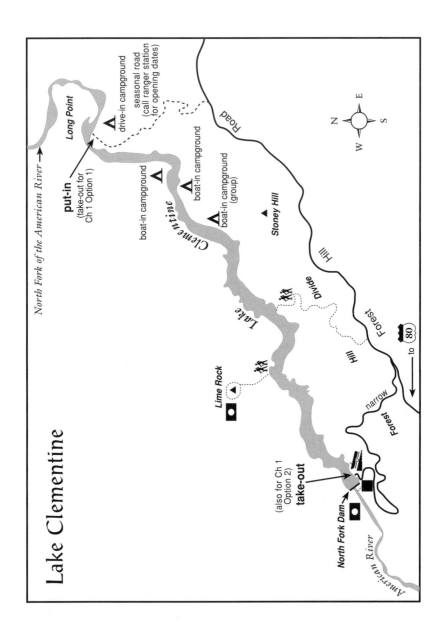

North Fork of the American River →

Long Point

put-in
(take-out for
Ch 1 Option 1)

drive-in campground

seasonal road
(call ranger station
for opening dates)

boat-in campground

boat-in campground

boat-in campground
(group)

Clementine

Lake

Stoney Hill

Divide

Hill

Forest

to (80)

narrow

Forest

Lime Rock

North Fork Dam

(also for Ch 1
Option 2)
take-out

American River

Road

N
W · E
S

PADDLING AREA 2:
Lake Clementine (North Fork Lake)

Trip Length: 4 miles one way

Maps: **USGS Topographic Quadrants:**
Auburn Quadrangle, 7.5 minute series
Greenwood Quadrangle, 7.5 minute series
USGS 1:250 000 Series: Sacramento, CA

Northern California Atlas & Gazetteer, Delorme Map Co.,
1996 edition, grid #87

Access: From Sacramento, take I-80 East to Auburn and go off at the
Forest Hill Road exit. Head east. Cross the new bridge overlooking
the North Fork of the American River gorge. The turnoff for lower
Lake Clementine and the dam is 3.2 miles from I-80. Drive another
mile on Forest Hill Road for the turnoff leading to the upper lake and
campground.

Difficulty: This is a classic flat-water paddle on a gem of a finger
lake created by a pour-over debris dam. The lake is approximately
four miles in length and quite narrow. The major risk involves
having to fight the afternoon wind blowing up the river gorge. This
problem may be eliminated by putting in at the upper lake access
and paddling with the wind on the return leg. I found that if the

wind catches you while you are still on the upper lake, by hugging the west shoreline you are in a natural windbreak for most of the return paddle.

The only other warning pertains to the use of the lake by motor boats and water skiers. I recommend paddling this lake in the fall and early spring to avoid the noise and wakes created by these boaters.

The dam holding back the waters of the North Fork of the American River at Lake Clementine is defined as a debris dam, meaning that it was built solely for the purpose of keeping silt and debris (caused by hydraulic mining) from reaching the Sacramento River and its delta. Thus, the reservoir's water level remains constant, allowing the vegetation to grow down to the water's edge. This eliminates the "bathtub ring" effect that mars so much of the scenery at other reservoirs.

As mentioned earlier, the best time to paddle on Lake Clementine is spring or fall before the summer boaters and water skiers converge on, in, and under its waters. This is the time to see or photograph the many wildflowers and animals making their homes on the banks and hillsides of the lake. If you begin your paddle on the lower end of the lake, be sure to hike to the view area to catch a glimpse of the

Fall reflection

spectacular falls created by the river as it pours over the dam. If the lighting is right, you might catch a great photograph of the falls with a rainbow overhead.

Soon after you begin your paddle, look high to your left for an exposed section of gray limestone similar to the rock quarried at Cool. This outcrop is called "Lime Rock" or "Robber's Roost." For an interesting description of how this rock got its name and the geology of the area, read page 75 of *The American River, North, Middle & South Forks*, listed in the bibliography.

Erosion of the limestone has created numerous caves and shallow niches in the exposed rock. These natural caves serve as nesting sites for turkey vultures—a common sight over the skies of the reservoir.

If a hike to the rocky outcrop is in order, locate the small rocky point just below and slightly east of Lime Rock. Wedge your boat in the clearing between the tules, orient yourself with reference points across the lake and then hike up to the drainage located below the rock.

Lime Rock

Follow this drainage upward and you will come out onto the talus pile created by the eroding limestone. A series of deer trails run east west just below the main outcrop. These trails intersect the trail that circles Lime Rock. **Note:** Because the trail is steep, wear gloves to protect your hands from the sharp rocks and prickly leaves of the many oaks growing on the hillside. Wear appropriate footwear to provide support for your ankles.

As you continue, look for families of mallard ducks and adult Canada geese that use the brush and reeds on the reservoir's edge as cover and nesting places. In the early spring, you may be fortunate to hear the honking of the geese echoing off the side canyons as they call to each other in flight over the reservoir.

Not placed on any of the maps is a small island approximately 3/4 of the distance from the dam, just before the campsites. With a little luck and at the right time of year, you may find the small sandy beach all to yourself. This is a great spot for lunch or a break before continuing up to the narrow end of the lake.

Just past the island you come across the campsites that make this lake so popular with the boating crowd during the summer. The sandy sites are well chosen for their easy access and views of the lake or side canyons. Here the reservoir narrows and you soon feel the pull of the current as the lake ends and the river begins.

Looking up-river to river right you will see more of the exposed gray limestone. If you are carrying binoculars, look up to the caves and see if you can spot a nesting turkey vulture. If not, then look down into the water and see if you can spot some of the large trout swimming by the banks and shady spots.

The rocky bar used as a beach on river right is also your take-out and the location of the unimproved campground. Above the small rapid on the west side of the river you can see the large, flat cobble bar called Long Point. Beyond this bend flows the North Fork of the American River and the section previously described.

Mule deer

Other Sources:

A Boating and Trail Guide to the North and Middle Forks of the American River, prepared jointly by the Department of Boating and Waterways and the Department of Parks and Recreation (phone 916-445-2616)

The American River, North Middle & South Forks; published by PARC (Protect American River Canyons); 1989

Recreation Lakes of California; Dirksen & Reeves, Recreation Sales Publishing; 1986

Notes

Cattails

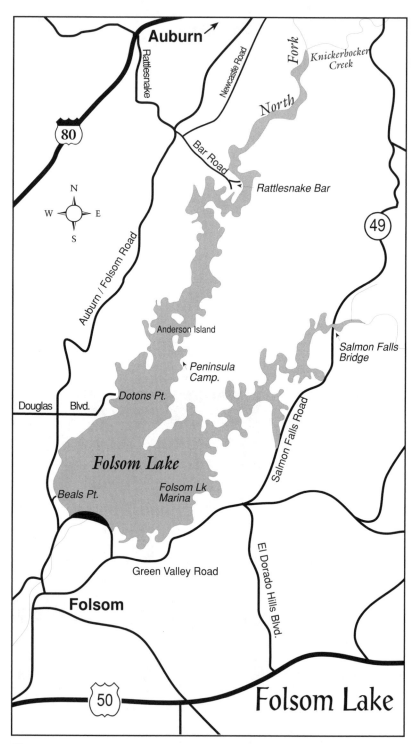

Folsom Lake

CHAPTER 3

The Sierra Foothills: Folsom Lake

The entire area of this arm of the lake was once the channel of the North Fork of the American River. In the late fall and spring, green grasses and wildflowers color the surrounding hills and ravines. You can hear the sounds of different migratory birds either flying overhead or on the water. Remnants of historical mining activity may be visited short distances from the water.

Loading up

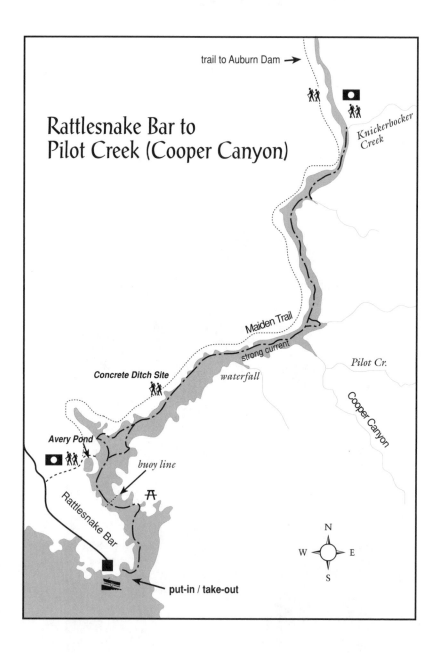

Rattlesnake Bar to
Pilot Creek (Cooper Canyon)

trail to Auburn Dam →

Knickerbocker Creek

Maiden Trail

strong current

Concrete Ditch Site

waterfall

Pilot Cr.

Cooper Canyon

Avery Pond

buoy line

Rattlesnake Bar

N
W ←◆→ E
S

put-in / take-out

Paddling Area 1: Rattlesnake Bar Boat Launch North to Pilot Creek (Cooper Canyon)

Trip Length: 6 miles round trip

Maps: USGS Topographic Quadrant:
Pilot Hill 7.5 minute series

Northern California Atlas & Gazetteer, DeLorme Mapping Co., 1988, grid #87

Access: From Sacramento, take Interstate 80 east. Exit and turn left on Horseshoe Bar Road. Stay on this road for approximately 3.5 miles. When you intersect Auburn-Folsom Road, turn left onto Auburn-Folsom Road. Drive for approximately 3 miles and turn right on Newcastle Road. After 1 mile the road splits and joins Rattlesnake Bar Road. Continue to the right on Rattlesnake Bar Road until you enter Folsom Lake Recreational Area. During the off-season, place your money in the "iron ranger" adjacent to the kiosk. To obtain current information on entry fees and other questions, call Auburn State Recreation Area, 916-367-2224.

To reach the boat ramp, drive past the kiosk and look for a boat launch sign with a directional arrow indicating a left turn onto a dirt side road. Continue on this road until you end at the launch ramp

Picnic spot near Avery Pond

approximately 1/2 mile from the turnoff. **(Note:** If the water level is below the ramp and all you see is mud, drive back on the same road and make a left approximately 0.2 mile from the launch ramp parking area. Cross over the small creek and angle to your left. The small cove in front of you has numerous fingers that allow a put-in. You can either portage down to the water or, if your vehicle has a high enough clearance, route-find a path closer to the water.)

Difficulty: The ever-present afternoon canyon wind blowing up the channel will be the main challenge to paddlers on this stretch of the lake.

During the winter flood season, water drawn down from the dam makes for a difficult and even impossible launch due to the deep mud between the launch ramp and the water. This low-water condition also exposes the lower North Fork channel of the American River. Subsequently, a strong current is created that is better suited as a workout than a recreational paddle. However, if the water level is high enough to cover the original river channel, go ahead and launch and be assured of a comfortable paddle as far a Mormon Ravine.

   If the water level is high enough to proceed, paddle up the channel. After leaving the boat launch and passing the small cove on channel left, look up. The twisted metal and concrete hanging over the water is all that's left of the flume belonging to the south canal, just one of the extensive water-carrying systems once used for hydraulic mining. If you drove to the lake using the directions provided, you passed a canal called the Boardman Canal. There is a more extensive and better preserved concrete remnant farther up the channel.

   If you are doing this paddle on a warm day in spring, the first cove on your left has a granite beach suitable for swimming or enjoying the view of the lush hills to the east. On the right side, as you begin the first bend in the channel, there is a narrow finger partially covered with the drowned tips of willows. The oak-covered hills beyond the inlet make for a nice hike or picnic spot. The shady areas around the oaks and pines are home to many small plots of wild iris and other wildflowers. **(Note:** If you are carrying a copy of Folsom Lake Map by Fish-N-Map Co., note that just above the 10-mile marker is a buoy line indicating a 5mph speed zone. From here on, your paddle should be without the stress from cross wakes caused by jet skis and motor boats.)
   Approximately 1 mile from the boat launch on the left is Mormon Ravine. Beach your boat on the sand at the mouth of the creek and

Fall reflections

hike up to the tree line beyond the scrape zone of the reservoir. Angle left following the rocky outcrop exposed at the mouth of Mormon Creek and hike up past the trees alongside the scrape zone. You should now be gazing on Avery's Pond, a gem of a small pond nestled amongst the oaks and Digger Pine trees.

If you hike to the south of the pond, you will cross the overgrown earthen dam that keeps the pond from draining into Folsom Reservoir. On the opposite side of the dam you can see the concrete ditch that was probably utilized for the distribution of water. The main path you pick up after you cross the small footbridge is part of the hiking/equestrian trail that follows the entire reservoir.

Once you complete the hike around the pond, take the trail that leads you to the mouth of Mormon Creek. Look for a large (Volkswagen-sized) flat slab of granite. The granite sits just above the scrape zone overlooking the mouth of Mormon Ravine. You will recognize the site because of the six small holes ground into the slab's surface. These holes are bedrock mortars, used for grinding seeds and acorns by the local Native Americans who originally inhabited the area. Even with all the changes that took place here, it isn't hard to let your imagination run wild and paint a mental picture of the place when local Native Americans gathered here to collect the ripening acorns and seeds from the pines.

When you continue the paddle, as you pass upstream of Mormon Ravine, look back at the small cove on the opposite shore. The size and depth of the silt covering what used to be a river bar is a good indicator of the amount of sediment being deposited into the main reservoir by each arm of the American River.

When I paddled this stretch of the reservoir in early March, I hiked up the small granite outcropping directly opposite the mouth of Mormon Ravine. Nestled in the coolness of the surrounding ground cover was a good-sized spread of wild iris.

Mortars

If the water level of the reservoir is down, you will come upon the first rapid, located a small distance above Mormon Ravine. It is here that, at low water, the first large gravel island separates the channel into two parts. The main channel is to the left of the island. This is also the extent of your paddle, unless you portage around or line the boat above the rapid. If the water level is high enough to cover the rapid, proceed up the channel to Pilot Creek.

No matter what choice you make, before leaving this spot, hike up the exposed layers of stratified bedrock to the trees above the scrape zone. A concrete ditch running parallel to the former river below is the canal mentioned earlier in this description. If you follow the ditch downstream (west), you will intersect the equestrian and hiking trail and come upon a large clearing overlooking the reservoir below. At the very edge of the scrape zone, you will find the remnant of a building. Take the time to study the small gnarled trees surrounding the "house" site. Yes, the two small trees are citruses! Depending on the time of year you do this paddle, you may spot a couple of scraggly oranges growing on the trees.

Assuming that the water level of the reservoir is high enough to permit a comfortable paddle beyond Mormon Ravine, the last phase of the trip will include a view of cascading waterfalls and paddling through a small, narrow gorge before beaching on river right at the mouth of Knickerbocker Creek.

The waterfalls are located on your right as you paddle up the channel. Look for cascading water flowing through the rocky debris at the entrance to a small canyon before you see them. To view the falls, beach your boat and hike over a lip of rock that covers the mouth of the canyon.

Feeling the tug of the current as you paddle upstream from the falls indicates the start of the narrow gorge and the final part of the trip.

Depending on the strength of the current, you may beach the boat at the downstream side of Pilot Creek, or among the rocks on river right. On a hot spring day, I hike to the first large pool and enjoy a swim in the clear but cold water. After a period of heavy rains, the hike up-canyon becomes impassable due to the heavy runoff from the creek.

From this canyon on, the reservoir ends and the river begins. If you are interested in hiking the Maidu Trail paralleling the river, ferry across and beach your boat on the large sandy bar at the bend above Pilot Creek. You should pick up the river trail at the high-water line. If you are adventurous, then visit the site of the controversial Auburn Dam site 8 miles up-river.

The strong current will give you a boost when you begin the return leg of the paddle. As you approach Mormon Ravine, stay to river right to miss the blast of a strong headwind. Remember, you will not have to worry about water-skiers or jet boats until you pass the buoy markers below the site of the ridge marking the location of Avery's Pond.

Other Sources:

Camanche Reservoir / Folsom Lake, FHS MAPS, Map #A-135, Folsom Lake, 1995

Folsom Lake, Family Fun Guide No. 1, Family Fun Publications, Map S/E-30

Sacramento County Street Guide and Directory, Thomas Guide, 1996 ed.

Avery Pond

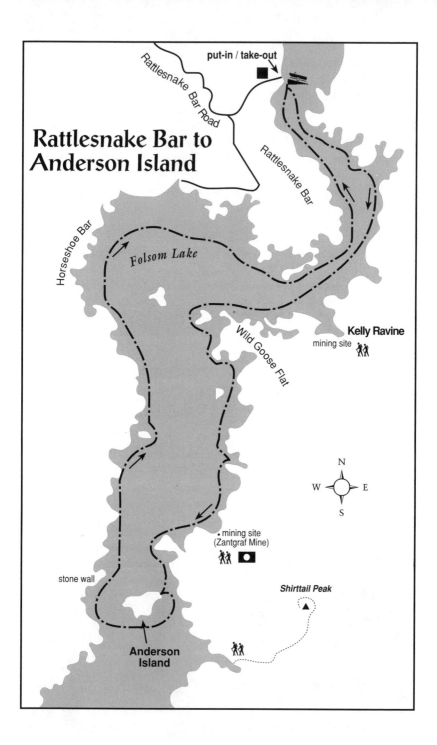

Rattlesnake Bar to Anderson Island

put-in / take-out

Rattlesnake Bar Road

Rattlesnake Bar

Horseshoe Bar

Folsom Lake

Wild Goose Flat

Kelly Ravine
mining site

mining site
(Zantgraf Mine)

stone wall

Shirttail Peak

**Anderson
Island**

N
W — E
S

North Arm of Folsom Lake

Paddling Area 2: Rattlesnake Bar Boat Launch South to Anderson Island

Trip Length: Round trip 7 miles

Maps: USGS Topographic Quadrant:
Pilot Hill, 7.5 minute series

Northern California Atlas & Gazetteer, DeLorme Mapping Co.,
1988, grid #87

Access: From Sacramento, take I-80 East. Exit and turn left on
Horseshoe Bar Road. Stay on this road for approximately 3.5 miles.
Turn left onto Auburn-Folsom Road. Drive for approximately 3 miles
and turn right on Newcastle Road. After 1 mile the road splits and
joins Rattlesnake Bar Road. Continue to the right on Rattlesnake Bar
Road until you enter Folsom Lake Recreational Area. During the off-
season, place your money in the "iron ranger" adjacent to the kiosk.
To obtain current information on entry fees and other questions, call
Auburn State Recreation Area, 916-367-2224.

To reach the boat ramp, drive past the kiosk and look for a boat launch sign with a directional arrow indicating a left turn onto a dirt side road. Continue on this road until you end at the launch ramp approximately 1/2 mile from the turnoff. (**Note:** If the water level is below the ramp and all you see is mud, drive back on the same road and make a left approximately 0.2 mile from the launch ramp parking area. Cross over the small creek and angle to your left. The small cove in front of you has numerous fingers that allow a put-in. You may either portage down to the water or, if your vehicle has a high enough clearance, route-find a path closer to the water.)

Difficulty: As mentioned in the previous Folsom Lake paddles, the wind presents the major hardship on the water. During spring and early summer, I have noticed that the wind usually, but not always, begins to blow around 10:00 a.m. and decreases after 5:00 p.m. On the plus side, you will have the wind on your back during the return leg of the paddle.

Follow the shoreline and keep a sharp eye out for rock outcrops just beneath the surface of the water. The rough granite may scrape and damage your boat before you realize your predicament. Occasionally, water skiers and jet boaters will speed by and their wakes may cause some discomfort.

This part of the lake has many points of interest to attract the paddler. On the opposite bank from the boat launch is Kelly Ravine. You may hike a short distance up the ravine to a hydraulic mining site. Piles of cobbles lie in mounds around the foundations of buildings and other mining debris.

Directly above the rock mounds and on top of the bluff is Wild Goose Flats. This scenic bluff contains a primitive boat-in campground.

A hiking trail leading away from the lake (easterly) parallels Kelly Ravine on the opposite bank, then climbs the ridge to connect with Rattlesnake Bar Road. A short distance from the campground, just off the trail to your left (north), look for a giant-size agave plant, also known as mescal or century plant. This locally-introduced species is the largest specimen I have seen in the wild.

For a more historic hike, cross over to the old road on the north side of Wild Goose Flats. This is the remains of the old Rattlesnake Bar Road that crossed over the bridge whose concrete embankments may be seen at low water between Kelly Ravine and Wild Goose Flats.

As you continue with the paddle, look out on the water for small diving birds with dark backs, white underbellies, and elongated

Kelly Ravine hydraulic mining site

necks. These are the western grebes which are master divers, but clumsy on land.

Long before you see them, the distinctive "honk" of the Canada geese will draw your attention to grassy high spots on the shore. These are the grazing areas for small families of geese that make the lake their home. One goose stands watch as the others feed. When you approach too closely, the honking warns the rest of the band to take flight or waddle to a more distant area.

Continue straddling the shoreline and look for signs of churning and splashes among the drowned vegetation at the water's edge. You are witnessing schools of carp breeding and laying their eggs in the warm waters of the shallows.

The Pilot Hill quadrangle topographic map, section 16, shows a symbol for a mine tunnel or cave entrance. I have searched for the mouth to this mine or cave, but without success. I have come across concrete foundations for what may have been a stamp mill or ore hopper, and smaller foundations that were for a building of some kind.

A more interesting historic site, located above the high-water line at the northwest base of Shirttail Peak, is the remnant of the Zantgraff mining operation. "(The mine) . . . was first worked in 1888 with a 10 stamp mill, which was increased to twenty stamps during the 1890's. By 1901 the production reached about one million dollars. The stamp mill and settlement were destroyed by fire in 1931." (*California Gold Camps,* pp. 265–266)

What looks like a small overgrown hill by the right side of the stream and at the base of Shirttail Peak is actually the toe of the large talus pile belonging to the Zantgraff Mine Shaft.

In the springtime, this hillside and the field in front of the mine is covered with a blanket of assorted wildflowers. The small stream has undercut the talus pile, exposing baseball-sized cobbles of milky white bull quartz. Hiking up the stream bed, you will come to the concrete remains of what may have been a diversion dam. Above it, look for a trail leading up the talus. Follow it, avoiding the poison

Anderson Island

oak, and you will spot the entrance to the mine shaft. A fallen digger pine has partially covered the mine, but you still have a limited view inside. The heavy overgrowth makes the ground extremely treacherous. Be careful and do not get too close to the deep entrance.

Looking around, you will see the remains of the stamp mill and buildings that were all part of this operation. It is hard to imagine that at one time this mine was producing a million dollars worth of gold annually.

A favorite lunch and view spot of mine is at the end of the talus slope. The dead pine at the edge of the slope makes for a comfortable backrest as you look out toward the lake. Looking up, you see soaring turkey vultures taking advantage of the thermals generated by the nearby peak and lake. With binoculars, you may view the cluster of mines and their talus piles grouped just below the northern tip of Shirttail Peak.

Hidden from view by the brush on the southwest side of the mine is the road leading to the top of Shirttail Peak and the mines described in the paddle from Dotons Point to Anderson Island. I suspect that this road was originally a wagon road, widened during the construction of the dam, and now a hiking trail.

To avoid the wind on the return paddle, cross over to the western shore. If time permits, aim for a small bay directly across from Anderson Island. Look for a stone wall at the base of the cove, the best preserved stone architecture within this section of the lake.

In the Eddy

Before Folsom Dam was completed, the North Fork of the American River ran through here as a pristine white water river. *A River I Remember*, by Jim L. White provides a wonderful account of what it was like to run this stretch of river during the 1950s in " . . . single seat, home built 15 foot canvas kayaks."

Other Sources:

Camanche Reservoir / Folsom Lake. Fish-n-Map Co. FHS MAPS (Fishing Hot Spots Inc.), map # A-135, Folsom Lake, 1995

Folsom Lake. Family Fun Guide no. 1, Family Fun Publications, Map no. S/E-30

Recreational Lakes of California. Dirksen and Reeves, Recreational Sales Publishing, 1996

Because this area has some points of historical interest, a short list of written sources is included to provide you with additional information on these localities:

Historic Spots in California: Three Volumes in One, by Mildred Brooke Hoover, Eugene Rensch Hero and Ether Grace Rensch, Stanford University Press, revised edition, 4th printing, 1962

California Gold Camps, Erwin G. Gudde, University of California Press

"A River I Remember," by Jim L. White, *Sierra Heritage Magazine,* May / June 1991. To request a copy of this article telephone the magazine at 916-823-3986.

Sacramento: Excursions Into Its History and Natural World, by William M. Holden, 1987 ed. (pp. 473–477)

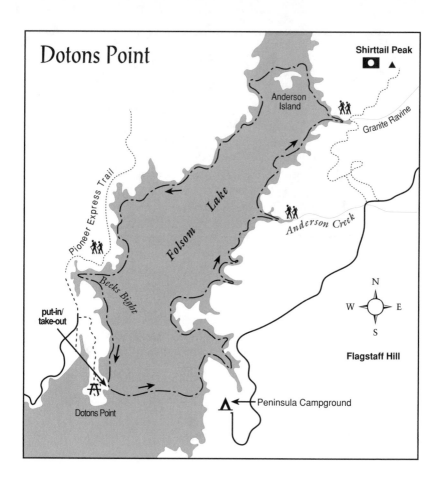

Dotons Point

Shirttail Peak

Anderson Island

Granite Ravine

Folsom Lake

Anderson Creek

Pioneer Express Trail

Beeks Bight

put-in/take-out

N
W E
S

Flagstaff Hill

Peninsula Campground

Dotons Point

PADDLING AREA 3:
Dotons Point North to Anderson Island

Trip Length: Five miles round trip.

Maps: **USGS Topographic Quadrants:**
Rocklin 7.5 minute series
Pilot Hill 7.5 minute series

Northern California Atlas and Gazetteer, Delorme Mapping Co.,
1995, grid #87

Note: Check with Folsom Lake Recreation Area for the availability of
free maps and brochures of the area. Their phone number is
916-988-0205.

Access: From Sacramento, take I-80 East to Douglas Boulevard in
Roseville. Exit east on Douglas Boulevard and follow it for approximately 4.5 miles to the main entrance to Folsom Lake at Granite Bay.

To get to Dotons Point, continue on the main park road. You will
pass Granite Bay main beach area and come to a Y-intersection.
Follow the sign pointing left toward Beeks Bight and Dotons Point.
A final right turn before Beeks Bight will end in a cleared area of

Launch at Dotons Point

high ground overlooking the lake. This is Dotons Point and your parking area. If your vehicle has a high clearance or you are willing to take a chance, drive down to the water's edge for a closer put-in.

Difficulty: THE WIND! This section of the lake has strong winds that come up in the afternoon and blow up the channel.

Speeding boaters may present a problem. In the fall and winter months, skiers and personal water craft are replaced by the speeding wakes of bass fishermen jetting to some special spot in search of lunkers.

As you begin this paddle, look across the lake and spot the road leading down to a camping area called Peninsula Campground. This is a great spot for a weekend stay. The site contains 100 camp spots, some with flush toilets and piped water. In the spring and fall the crowds are gone and you can pick a site with an exceptional view of the lake.

Stay close to the bank and you will be able to spot the Canada geese that feed on the grasses along the shore. Browsing deer and an occasional coyote scavenging the water line may make for a memorable moment.

The geology of the area is readily discernible due to the scraping off of the soils and the ground cover. The sun glistening on crystals of quartz cast bright flashes as you paddle by. Take the time to stop and examine the minerals. You will see small clear or milky crystals formed in cavities within the quartz.

Just across the northernmost boat launch at Peninsula Campground is a small primitive campground. It's a perfect overnight spot for canoeists and kayakers.

The next major ravine on the map, and noticeable from the water, is Anderson Creek. Paddle through the willows and beach your boat on any exposed sandy spot. Hike the stream until you intersect an old wagon road running north and south. This is part of the hiking trail that follows the lake from Wild Goose Flats then intersects Line Quarry Road above upper Anderson Creek. It skirts the high ground above Deep Ravine to follow the shoreline of the South Fork arm of Folsom Lake. (For more detailed coverage of the trails, see the *Camanche Reservoir / Folsom Lake Map* by **Fish-n-Map Co.**, listed in the bibliography.) A short hike along the trail may reward you with some great views of the lake and spotting, or at least hearing, a wild turkey (the feathered kind).

As you continue with the paddle, head for the rounded ridge on

Shirttail Peak

the northeast side of the lake with a road running around it. This is Shirttail Peak. Paddle toward the small inlet to a creek on the same side of the peak. On the maps the creek flows through Granite Ravine. Before you reach the inlet, you will pass small floating houses on the water with the names of SS RELIEF. They are for your hygienic convenience and not to be confused with a floating picnic or camping site.

Beach your boat as close to the stream rushing out of the ravine as you can. If exploring Granite Ravine, be sure to wear hiking boots or other ankle-supported style of footwear. This hike leads you to some beautiful, clear pools and small but picturesque waterfalls. If you time it right, clusters of assorted wildflowers will be blooming along the streambed.

Just below the first set of falls are a series of nice pools that are interspersed by ribbons of swift running water. This is the home of John Muir's favorite bird, the water ouzel (*The Wilderness World of John Muir*, pp. 147–161). Take a moment to watch as it dives into the fast stream and disappears underwater.

SS Relief

Eventually, the little bird will pop out, fly to a nearby rock and surprise you with its long flutelike song.

If, on the other hand, you decide to hike up the road toward Shirttail Peak, you will be rewarded with a spectacular view of Folsom Lake and the surrounding foothills. From up here you may watch turkey vultures and hawks as they soar over the shoreline below. I have startled deer and, in turn, was spooked by a coyote that was under a large manzanita shrub watching my beleaguered progress up the trail.

Just before reaching the summit and the adjacent mine shafts, you will come upon exposed islands of weathered rock. The patterns of red, yellow and orange lichen create intricate designs on the rock surfaces.

Upon reaching the summit, several talus piles provide evidence of former mining activity in the area. The main shaft is off on your left facing northwest as you approach on the road/trail. Smaller shafts dot the area but are overgrown with a dense cover of manzanita. The road you are hiking eventually intersects Lime Quarry Road that ends at the Peninsula Campground.

If you are fortunate enough to be paddling in the spring or in a time of high water, paddle through the small inlet on the southeast side of Anderson Island. Here you will find a small rookery of great blue herons. Please do not approach too closely or you will stress the adult birds. I have managed to take some great photos while observing the birds from the small point of land rounding the south shore of the lake adjacent to the island.

If the herons are not nesting, take the time to hike the small island. Stay on the game trails or you may blunder into poison oak that grows in dense thickets under the cool shade of the oaks. I have come across several turkeys using an old pine snag that provides a clear view of the surrounding area.

On your return leg of the paddle you will face a stiff headwind. So, to minimize your struggle, cross to the west side of the lake channel and follow the shoreline back to your vehicle. As you paddle along this side of the lake you will notice a trail following the high-water line of the lake. This is the historic Western States Pioneer Express Trail that connects Carson City, Nevada to Sacramento. One of the indicators for the location of the trail is the stacked rock embankments built to keep the trail from eroding and sliding.

At Beek's Bight, paddle through the drowned willows and keep a sharp eye out for cluster of wild iris that grow near the shore. After you pass the picnic area located in a small cove, you should spot your vehicle at the take-out beach.

Stone embankment on Pioneer Express Trail

Other Sources:

Comanche Reservoir / Folsom Lake, Fish-n-Map Co.

Folsom Lake, Map # A-135, FHS Maps

Folsom Lake, Map #S / E-30, Family Fun Publication

Recreation Lakes of California, Dirksen and Reeves, Recreation Sales
    Publishing, 1996

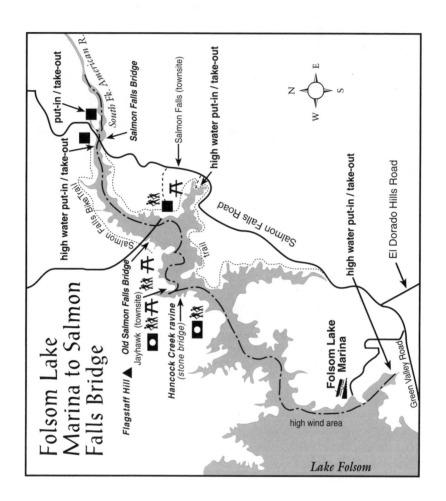

Folsom Lake Marina to Salmon Falls Bridge

put-in / take-out

South Fk. American R.

Salmon Falls Bridge

Salmon Falls (townsite)

high water put-in / take-out

high water put-in / take-out

Salmon Falls Bike Trail

trail

Salmon Falls Road

high water put-in / take-out

El Dorado Hills Road

Flagstaff Hill ▲ **Old Salmon Falls Bridge**
Jayhawk (townsite)

Hancock Creek ravine
(stone bridge)

Folsom Lake Marina

Green Valley Road

high wind area

Lake Folsom

N E S W

CHAPTER 4

The Sierra Foothills:
Highway 50 Corridor

PADDLING AREA 1:
Folsom Lake Marina (Brown's Ravine)
to Salmon Falls Bridge

Trip Length: 4.5 miles one way

Maps: USGS Quadrants:
Clarksville, 7.5 minute series
Pilot Hill, 7.5 minute series

Northern California Atlas & Gazetteer, DeLorme Mapping Co., 1996, grid #87

Access: The launch area for this trip is the Folsom Lake Marina in Brown's Ravine (also known as Mormon Bar). For current entrance fees and paddling conditions phone 916-933-1300.

To get there from Sacramento, take Highway 50 East. Exit at El Dorado Hills Boulevard, and continue north for 4 miles. Make a left turn on Green Valley Road and drive approximately 0.6 mile. Make a right turn at the sign for the marina turnoff.

If the water level is low, follow the signs and launch your boat at Hobie Ramp. If the water level is high enough, consider a shuttle up to Salmon Falls Bridge. To get there, backtrack onto Green Valley Road and make a left turn. Stay on Green Valley Road for approximately 1/2 mile. Turn left onto Salmon Falls Road, and follow it for approximately 6 miles. Cross over the new Salmon Falls Bridge, and make a right turn into the Skunk Canyon parking area. You may also use the parking facility on your left just before crossing the bridge.

Difficulty: Although this is considered a flatwater paddle similar to the ones described on the arm of the old North Fork channel, the lake's water level plays an important role in determining the extent of the paddle before either taking-out or turning back. A low water level brings back the flow in the old river channel. This, in turn, creates a current that becomes extremely difficult to negotiate at the vicinity of the old Salmon Falls Bridge.

See the Pilot Hill Quad, section 35 and the Sweetwater Creek / Folsom Lake Map; Fish-n-Map Co., mile marker 7.0. (Sources listed at end of Paddline Area text.)

The first mile, from the Folsom Lake Marina to the entrance of the channel at the 4-mile marker, is extremely windblown. The prevailing north wind blowing across the lake builds wavelets that strike the boat abeam. Furthermore, the wind is pushing against the boat's stern. This continuous combination of wind and breaking waves against your boat will not only tire you but could also cause the boat to broach. Once you enter the upper channel past the 4-mile marker, the surrounding hills block all but the strongest wind gusts.

The South Fork channel is historically fascinating, with its remnants of mining activity and small but poignant clutters of man's attempt to amass riches from the river. This is the most varied of the paddles within Folsom Lake.

If you are a white-water enthusiast, you may run a rare white water after a heavy release from Folsom Dam. During extremely wet winters, the Bureau of Reclamation, in an attempt to anticipate heavy runoff, lowers the lake to near-drought conditions. The subsequent emergence of the South Fork channel once again beckons boaters with intermediate skills to negotiate the rapids of a formerly drowned section of river. Beyond the old Salmon Falls bridge, the channel once again is claimed by the slack waters of the lake. Paddling against the current, you can feel the diminished strength of the river as you lean forward and put that extra little bit of effort into your strokes.

For a more traditional touring excursion, put in at the marina and spend the day exploring the interesting ravines as you paddle to the old bridge. In the fall, just before the water level is drawn down, I start my paddle at the small pond located on the left side of the kiosk, just as you enter the marina. Behind the grove of willows are white egrets, great blue herons, and other bird species.

Paddle past the main launch area, bank right and aim for the narrow channel. This is the entrance to the South Fork arm of the lake. From this point on, until you enter the confines of the channel, be wary of the wind. Once you leave the wide bay behind, you may decide to explore the smaller coves and drowned ravines of former creeks that drained into the preexisting river. I have spent an entire day examining the three or four side canyons located down the lake from Deep Ravine.

Many species of birds, deer, and other animals use these smaller ravines to seek food or shelter. On one occasion, I have come across a lone coyote, its nose to the shoreline. It was so intent on searching for food that I gained a moment to study its antics before it noticed my presence. With a surprised yelp and jump, the coyote disappeared over the ridge and into the oaks that mark the edge of the reservoir's high waterline.

A note of caution: When exploring the side bays and inlets if you use maps to guide your way into these side channels, be aware that lower water levels change the features of the terrain to the point where it is easy to misidentify your location. My friend Lisa and I mistook the main channel for Deep Ravine (one of the larger drowned creek canyons).

A good place to stretch your legs and hike is located in the first small U-shaped inlet south of Deep Ravine. Look for the trail on the upper right bank just above the high-water mark. The trail, wide enough to be called a road, leads up the ridge to intersect with the Peninsula Ridge Trail, the main hiking trail, approximately 1/2 mile from the lake.

The trail takes you up to a small ridge where you will hike through a woodland of mossy oaks and digger pines. If hiking in winter, you will be treated to the sight of many western bluebirds flitting from tree to tree in search of insects. Take the time to inspect the trunks and branches of the oak trees. The thousands of neatly drilled holes are the work of the acorn woodpecker. Some of the holes contain acorns stuffed inside: "One tree was estimated to have 50,000 acorns imbedded in the trunk . . . " (Picket, p. 82). For a fascinating description on the life history of these social birds, read Verna Johnston's *California Forests and Woodlands*, pp. 85–87.

Upon reaching the top of the ridge, you are rewarded with a grand view of the channel leading into Deep Ravine as well as the upper arm of the lake.

After you complete the hike, paddle your boat into the small cove immediately above Deep Ravine. Beach the boat close to the mouth of the stream and walk up the ridge to intersect the hiking trail. This trail which follows the shoreline can be hiked all the way to Salmon Falls bridge. I have taken the trail to a small stream that flows into the lake and has a lively effervescent quality about it.

When you are back in your boat, paddle across the channel, around Iron Mountain and into the mouth of New York Creek Cove. You will recognize the location by the sight of the floating privies, appropriately named "SS Relief."

With the water level down you will pass exposed layers of silt beds that mask the preexisting terrain. Although this ugly mass of mud prevents the growth of plants and hides the area's history, when dry enough it becomes an open book, showing the passage of many animals. I have noted the tracks of deer, coyote, raccoon, goose, heron, and other smaller animals. An additional bonus was finding a complete fishing rod and reel—lure included!

Paddling farther, you will enter the exposed narrow bed of New York Creek. Hiking above the stream bed and looking down, you will notice the many rows of cobbles laid in some semblance of order. At one time this area was mined and the cobbles are the remains of that operation. Above the high-water line is another remnant of that period; the rusted metal skeleton of an old truck.

For those of you continuing on to the old Salmon Falls Bridge, do not miss the chance to explore Hancock Creek. As you approach the mouth of the creek, you must pass under a handsome stone bridge. There is a look of pride in the construction of this small architectural gem. Make your approach from a slight angle. The view of Hancock Creek framed by the bridge makes a picturesque sight.

Paddle your boat underneath the bridge and beach it. As you hike up the stream bed, look for carp that may be stranded by the receding waters.

stone bridge at Hancock Creek

In the Eddy

I was rather startled when placing my foot into a shallow pool: the water erupted with a splash and a large fish darted upstream. With this introduction, I began to study the pools and shallows with greater care. I noticed there were at least four or five more carp trying to survive. Their battered bodies gave testimony to their repeated attempts at escaping the punishing waters of the stream.

The overhead banks of silty mud made it impossible for me to scramble out of the streambed. Eventually, where the stream had washed off the mud creating a debris pile, I was able to hike to a level area above the creek. Looking upstream, I spotted a mound of green rock on the left side of the ravine. It turned out to be a talus pile adjacent to a filled mine shaft. The rusting steel trough further added to the evidence that mining activity occurred here.

Hearing voices, I looked up and saw a small group of cyclists negotiating a trail down from the adjacent ridge. Checking the map, I realized they were on the Salmon Falls Mountain Bike Trail, a trail completed only a few years ago and originating at the new Salmon Falls Bridge.

Startled by our presence, a small herd of Black Tail Deer bounded into the grove of oak surrounding the ravine. Overhead two hawks were attempting to disguise their presence by mingling with the Turkey Vultures hoping to fool the small game hiding in the brush.

Hiking back, I stayed above the stream bed and walked along the silt covered flats. Where small streamlets have cleared the mud, veins of sparkling, milky quartz shine in the sunlight. As the mud dries, it cracks into deep lines that resemble a huge canvas of an abstract painting.

Stay to the left as you paddle around the point of Hancock Creek Ravine. Look for the remains of an old wagon road that followed the stream and connected different mining communities within the now-drowned river canyon. Think of the labor involved in the shaping, carrying and placement of the stones that make up the roadbed!

The red soil appearing in the side walls of the river bank indicates that you are nearing the site of the old bridge. Just before you approach the bend in the channel, look for the large mud flat extending from the shore into the water on river left. The small hill beyond the mud is the location of a pioneer cemetery and the last remnant of the gold mining town named Jayhawk. If the mud is dry enough to support your weight, beach the boat and hike up the hill. As you get closer to the bank, pieces of old glass, china, and crockery can be spotted littering the ground. At the top of the hill are grave mounds.

In the late winter, the green grass provides a lovely carpet over the remains of the cemetery; springtime brings the wildflowers and domestic flowers that were planted at the grave sites. The last time I visited the area I counted thirteen rock grave mounds and three possible grave sites.

Looking northwest toward the lake channel, you may spot cairns of rock that resemble fallen walls. These rock piles may or may not be the remains of the town site.

An added bonus to the historical aspect of your hike is the magnificent view of the old bridge, the river, and the hills beyond. If you are standing on the hill during a sunny late afternoon, be sure to catch the salmon-colored light on the side walls of the cliffs. The large hill in the background with the road slashed diagonally along its flank is Flagstaff Hill. Looking south, you will spot a small forest of conifers planted in 1972 by the Institute of Forest Genetics (Placerville, CA) and the Pacific Southwest Research Station as an experimental forest project. Threading its way through the grove of trees is a section of the old Salmon Falls Road.

From this point on, the strong current will deter further upstream travel. You will have to paddle back toward Folsom Lake Marina. **(Note:** There is a parking area on the lower (south) end of Sweetwater Creek. You may access it from Salmon Falls Road. The exit is on your left approximately 3.5 miles from Salmon Falls Road and Green Valley Road junction. If the mud banks are dry, it may be possible to portage your boat to the parking area.)

In the Eddy

At the bend in the river, in what is now the upper South Arm of Folsom Lake, stood the gold mining town of Salmon Falls. Located on the present day mud flats at the mouth of Sweetwater Creek, the town was named after the nearby falls.

Before the town, the waterfalls were a well known fishing area where local Indians caught migrating salmon. In 1848, the area was mined by the Mormons. By 1850, the town was thriving with a population of three thousand.

Across the river, the smaller town of Jayhawk was built. Today, the only evidence of these communities are the overgrown pioneer cemeteries on nearby hills.

On January 1, 1990, during a long period of drought, the water level of the lake dropped so far as to revive the rapid. The entire stretch of river, from the new Salmon Falls Bridge down to Mormon Island, became runnable white water.

True to form, a small group of experienced local white water kayakers ran the emergent rapid, one more time.

Site of original Salmon Falls Rapid

Other Sources:

Camanche Reservoir / Folsom Lake. Fish-n-Map Co.

Folsom Lake Fishing Boating Map. FHS Maps, Map #A-135, 1995

Recreational Lakes of California. Dirksen and Reeves, Recreational Sales
   Publishing, 1996 ed.

Old Salmon Falls Bridge

Notes

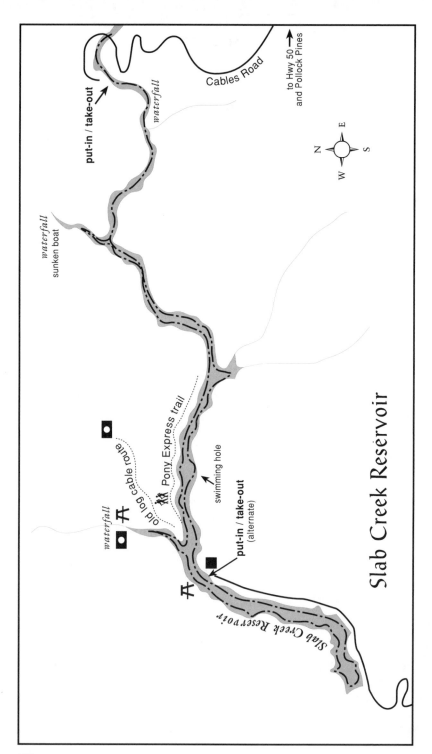

Slab Creek Reservoir

put-in / take-out

waterfall

Cables Road

to Hwy 50 and Pollock Pines

N E S W

waterfall
sunken boat

Pony Express trail

old log cable route

waterfall

waterfall

swimming hole

put-in / take-out
(alternate)

Slab Creek Reservoir

Paddling Area 2:
Slab Creek Reservoir

Trip Length: 9 miles round trip

Maps: USGS Topographical Quadrants:
Pollock Pines Quadrangle, 7.5 minute series
Slate Mountain Quadrangle, 7.5 minute series

Northern California Atlas and Gazetteer, DeLorme Mapping Co., grid #88

Access: From Sacramento, take Highway 50 East toward Lake Tahoe. Turn off at the Pollock Pines / Sly Park exit. At the stop sign make a left turn (north) and drive under Highway 50 to the next stop sign. Turn left onto Pony Express Trail. Drive past the Safeway store and parking lot. Look for a small street on your right named Forebay Road. Turn right and follow Forebay Road for approximately seven miles. As you twist and turn on this roller coaster of a road, it merges somewhere around four miles and becomes Cable Road. (If you try to find a road sign instead of concentrating on your driving, it's a safe bet that you and your vehicle will become airborne.)

As you descend into the gorge of the South Fork of the American River, the road becomes extremely narrow. Be careful of vehicles around the tight bends and deer that use the road as a crossing point. (**Note:** If you are making the drive in spring or after a spell of cold weather, be especially cautious; the road becomes icy when you enter the inner gorge.)

Eventually the road drops down to the river and crosses over the south fork bridge. To your right is the SMUD / PG & E powerhouse. If an emergency occurs, someone working at the powerhouse may be of help. Turn left immediately after crossing the bridge and follow the dirt path adjacent to the river bank until it dead-ends at the tail end of the reservoir. This is the put-in for the paddle on the reservoir. **Please note:** the amount of the flow in the river as it enters the lake. *If the current is very strong, do not launch your boat.*

Difficulty: Similar to the type of boating found on Lake Clementine. Wind blowing up the canyon in the afternoon may make the paddle difficult and tiresome. The strength of the current generated by the river's inflow into the lake may present a hazard to inexperienced boaters when attempting to ferry across on the return leg of the paddle.

Want the look and feel of paddling on a Canadian lake, but don't have the time to drive there? No problem! Have I got a boating spot for you!

Slab Creek Reservoir is a hidden jewel in the gorge of the upper South Fork of the American River. The reservoir is approximately 4.5 miles long and dammed by a small hydroelectric dam that controls the depth of the lake. The narrow, steep gorge with its numerous

Slab Creek Reservoir looking northeast from the Pony Express Road

bends bears a strikingly similar appearance to Lake Clementine. What makes this lake so special is its elevation. Nestled at a base of 3,000 feet, the surrounding evergreen forest grows down to the water's edge. The trees provide an atmosphere very similar to the fir-forested lakes of Canada and our own Northwest Coast.

The rock faces on the walls of the gorge are covered with lichen and miniature ferns. At one time these same rocks were part of an ancient sea floor and are now metamorphosed into schist and gneiss. Peering upward on the east side of the lake, tall rows of Douglas fir and other evergreens blanket the skyline almost the entire length of the lake. To the west, where the hills are composed of a different soil base and are exposed to the sun more, clusters of digger pine and manzanita predominate.

Paddling down the lake, the canyon slowly widens, allowing light and the warmth of the sun to reach the water. If you are paddling the reservoir after a rain, you get an additional treat—the sound and sight of numerous waterfalls cascading down the steep slick-rock.

Just before you reach Cable Point, look to your right (north) and you can see the remains of the old Pony Express road angling downward from the top of the ridge and disappearing into the lake. The trek to the top of the ridge rewards the hiker with a spectacular view of the drowned river gorge and the lake that fills it. The last time I was here, I was treated to the sight of a deer swimming across the reservoir and then slowly walking into the forest.

Slab Creek Reservoir

Upon reaching Cable Point, you are approximately three miles from the put-in. Look to your right and the remnants of a former logging cable operation can be seen carved into the hillside. From here, you can continue to paddle to the dam or explore some of the side canyons and trails that are nearby.

Pony Express Road

Other Sources:

El Dorado National Forest, US Forest Service Map

Metsker's *El Dorado County Map*

The Thomas Guide, El Dorado County, 1997 ed.

Notes

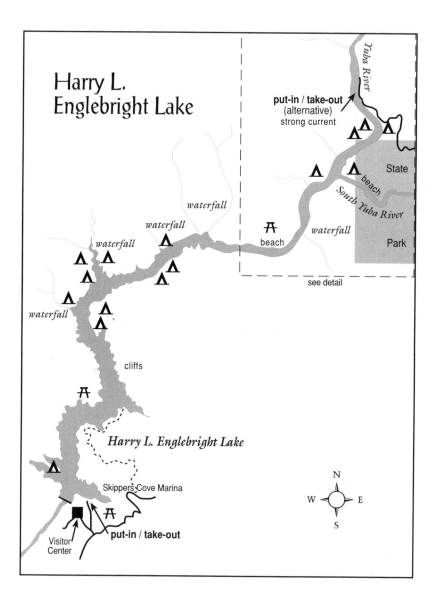

Harry L. Englebright Lake

put-in / take-out
(alternative)
strong current

Yuba River

State

beach

South Yuba River

waterfall

beach

waterfall

Park

see detail

waterfall

waterfall

waterfall

waterfall

cliffs

Harry L. Englebright Lake

Skippers Cove Marina

put-in / take-out

Visitor
Center

N
W ⊕ E
S

CHAPTER 5

The Sierra Foothills:
Highways 49 / 65 Corridors
Northern Gold Fields

PADDLING AREA 1: Harry L. Englebright Lake

Trip Length: Contains 24 miles of shoreline stretched into a thin, sinuous lake. The round-trip paddle to the mouth of the South Yuba River and back to the parking area requires a full day.

Maps: **USGS Topographical Quadrants:**
French Coral, CA, 7.5 minute series
Oregon House, CA, 7.5 minute series
Smartville, CA, 7.5 minute series

Northern California Atlas and Gazetteer, grid #79, section B-4.5

Access: Part of the fun of paddling on Lake Englebright is driving there. No matter what route you take, they all go through some of the finest scenery covering California's foothills. In addition, you also wind through a portion of the northern gold fields and view some of the historical sites as well.

The first and most direct route is to take I-5 North to State Highways 99 / 70 North. At the 99 / 70 split, continue on 70 into Marysville and take California State Highway 20 east toward Grass Valley. After driving for approximately 20.5 miles, you come to the junction of Smartville Road and Highway 20. Continue for 1/2 mile on Highway 20, and make a left turn onto Moony Flat Road. (**Note:** This is a rough, narrow two-lane road. Please watch your speed when driving through the small community of Moony Flat.)

After 3 miles, look to your left for the sign that says The Narrows Boat Launch and Visitor's Center. If you need to obtain supplies, continue on Moony Flat Road and make the next turn leading to Skipper's Cove Marina.

Upon entering the Narrows facility, you pass the parking area for boat trailers and overnight parking. Continue down the steep and very narrow two-lane road. When you reach the small fork, a left turn will take you to the restrooms and visitor's center. If you continue straight, you will pass the boat launch ramp and eventually the day use parking and picnic area. As of 1997, use of the boat launch requires a $2.00 fee per boat. (**Note:** To avoid the stress of trying to launch the boats from this area while other larger motorized craft are also being driven into the water, hand-launch from the picnic area. You may use the small loading dock to launch from.)

The second route to Englebright Lake involves taking I-80 east into Auburn. Pick up State Highway 49 North until you reach the town of Grass Valley, then continue on State Highway 20 West. Turn right onto Moony Flat Road and drive for 3 miles. Turn into the entrance of the lake. This route takes you through the historical gold country of the northern gold fields.

For the more adventuresome and those with time on their hands, try this route: from Sacramento, take I-80 East and exit onto California State Highway 65. Drive for 18 miles into the town of Sheridan. Turn right on Camp Far West Road. Skirt around Camp Far West Reservoir. Upon crossing the bridge at the reservoir's dam turn right. You are still on Camp Far West road (on some maps the road is called Long Road) which eventually becomes Waldo Road after you cross the historic Waldo Bridge (built in 1901) at Dry Creek. (**Note:** Waldo Road is a rough gravel road. While it is possible to drive on it with any type of vehicle, be prepared to "shake, rattle and roll!")

Stay on this road for approximately 6 miles until you intersect Hammonton-Smartville Road. Turn right, drive for 1 mile and exit onto California State Highway 20. Make a right turn, drive 1/2 mile and make a left onto Moony Flat Road. Using this route, you will be driving and bouncing through the Spenceville Wildlife Management and Recreation Area. Try to time your drive in the early morning or late afternoon. The detour is worth the drive because of the scenery of the oak woodlands and the variety of wildlife. Small herds of deer and families of wild turkeys may be seen browsing and strolling in the grasslands. Coyotes scamper among the oaks as you approach, and woodpeckers flit from tree to tree in their distinctive flight pattern. Take time to stop

Waldo Bridge

and explore Dry Creek. If you are here in the summer, enjoy the tart taste of the many blackberries growing along the creek bed.

Those with a high clearance vehicle can take advantage of the rough unpaved road leading to the upper half of the lake at Rice's Crossing. The road may be washed out or impassable at times so call ahead to the ranger station at Bridgeport 916-432-2546, or CalTrans 800-427-7623 for road conditions.

Difficulty: Stiff headwinds and cross wakes from a variety of motorized craft are the main source of discomfort in paddling the lake.

No matter what time of day you launch your boat on Englebright Lake, the first thing you will notice is the golden light on the surrounding foothills, followed by the abrupt change to the darker hues of shimmering water. As you prepare to launch the boat, you get a wonderful telescopic view descending along the length of the first gorge on the lake.

Wave good-bye to the curious inhabitants of the moored houseboats and paddle across the lake to the opposite shoreline. (**Note:** many of the houseboats are for rent. For additional information, call the marina at 916-639-2262.) Proceeding past the edge of the marina and the last of the houseboats, your best bet is to stay on the left (northwest) side of the lake until you reach Keystone Ravine. By paddling on the left side, you are in a good position to watch the unfolding of the steep layers of massed rock eroding out of the sides of Keystone Ravine. Within the cove of the ravine, you may see the first of many houseboats moored along a beach or swim area. Directly above the lake on the northern bluff are the buildings belonging to the Carmichael Ranch. As you continue past the ranch and the ravine, you will hear the sound of the first small waterfall hidden in a brushy stream bed.

Eventually you will spot the first easily visible boat camp site at Long's Cove. The majority of these camp sites are well planned and maintained. On this end of the lake, my favorite sites are Rocky Bluff and Long's Point camps. At Rocky Bluff, the sound and sight of a waterfall comes with the camp site.

Between Singles Point and Upper Boston Bar, the opportunity to land is slim due to the private property that fronts the shoreline. Eventually you pass a lovely shaded beach and camp on the left (north) shore. This is Bucks Beach. If you are lucky to find it open, take the opportunity to stop and take a break. Unfortunately, unless you are self-sustaining, i.e. carrying your own toilet, this site is for day use only.

Between Bucks Beach and the next site at Dixon Hill, you will paddle past numerous waterfalls on both sides of the lake—only one of which, in summer, may have enough cascading water to be heard or seen from the boat. As you make the approach toward Dixon Hill camp site, look up on the high northern hillside for a view of the sluice snaking its way through the trees. This is part of the Browns Valley Ditch, a feature going back to the days of constructing New Bullards Bar Reservoir.

Just past Dixon Hill on the right (south) is the mouth of the South Yuba River. You will spot a large sand and gravel bar on the right side

Lower campsite

of the river mouth. On my last paddle to this area, in the summer of 1997, there was a volleyball net set up by the Englebright Lake house boaters. Just beyond the mouth, you encounter the clear and cooler water of the South Yuba. At the first right bend of the

Boat-in campground

river, your upstream paddle ends at a small rapid. At low water, you can bow-surf your boat in the turbulent water.

On river left is a large sandy bar with a fine beach that slopes into a set of deep and clear pools. Beyond this bar the river makes a dogleg that leads to the historical site of the covered bridge at Bridgeport. If you have the time, secure your boat and hike up-river to the bridge. The hike is approximately 3/4 of a mile on a small but well used trail.

If you are boat camping, there is no camping allowed within the State Park boundary that begins past the mouth of the South Fork of the Yuba River. However, there are several campsites surrounding the river mouth. The first one called Dixon Hill is located on the left (north) side of the lake just before you reach the river mouth. The campsite location is next to an intermittent stream. By summer, the stream dries up, leaving behind pools of standing water and creating a breeding ground for mosquitoes. In addition, debris pushed by the wind piles up in the small beach that serves as the boat take-out area.

A more inviting campsite is located on the upper tip of the river mouth and the right (south) side of the lake. The area is called Point Defiance and has 8 secluded campsites. Several small but sandy beaches are also part of this location.

How the point was named is somewhat of a mystery. According to Chuck Scimeca, a California State Park Ranger at Bridgeport, Point Defiance was the location of a former bridge (not to be confused with the former bridge at Rice's Crossing). There seem to be a lot of former bridges on this stretch of the river. In addition to the bridge, the area was also the site of a Chinese community. Little else is known about the naming of the point.

Two other boat camping sites are found farther up the lake. Missouri Bar, the first one on the left (north) bank, is split into two sites. The main site of Missouri Bar contains 15 campsites; Lower Missouri Bar contains 4 sites.

The entire Missouri Bar campsite is visible from the water as a highly prominent built-up sand bar. A large and bushy willow tree growing on the sand bar may be used as a reference point. Although the site has many positive aspects, such as a great sandy beach, shade, good view down lake, and a breeze to blow away the bugs, the water is too cold for swimming. From here to Rice's Crossing, the lake comes under the influence of the Main Yuba River. Even in late summer, the current is swift and the water uncomfortably cold.

The last campsite on the lake, located on the right (south) bank is called Sunnyside and contains 2 sites. I found this campsite ideal for an individual or a small family. Its location provides ample seclusion and shade with a choice view of the lake. Again, the swiftness of the current and the coldness of the water precludes any swimming or bathing.

Waterfall

From Point Defiance to Rice's Crossing (the take-out for those of you who drove down the steep and rough road), the lake's influence is diminished and replaced by the personality of the Yuba River. In the spring, the current may be too strong to paddle against. This means that the last area for casual paddling is Missouri Bar.

By summer, as you round the bend past Sunnyside campsite, the channel opens onto a broad vista with a foreground view of the abutments that held the bridge at Rice's Crossing. On either side of the banks are stands of tall cotton-woods entangled with vines, and shadowy bushes of various shape and size. In the background are the evergreen bands of assorted pines and firs highlighting the contours of the steep ridge lines.

From here you may either take out at Rice's Crossing, turn back and paddle back to your campsite, or take a deep pull on the water bottle and start the long paddle back to your original put-in at the Narrows boat launch.

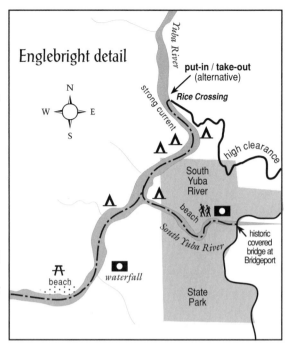

Other Sources:

Nevada & Sierra Counties, Compass Maps Inc., 1995 ed.

Pamphlets:

Englebright Lake Recreation Guide, US Army Corps of Engineers Sacramento District: CESPK BRO 360-1-21, Apr. 93

Outdoor Recreation Guide, Northern and Central California, US Army Corps of Engineers, Sacramento District: CESPK BRO 360-1-8, Jan. 94

Guidebooks:

Recreation Lakes of California, Recreation Sales Publishing, 1993, 10th ed., p. 50

California Boating and Water Sports, Foghorn Press, 1996, p. 220

Lower Yuba River

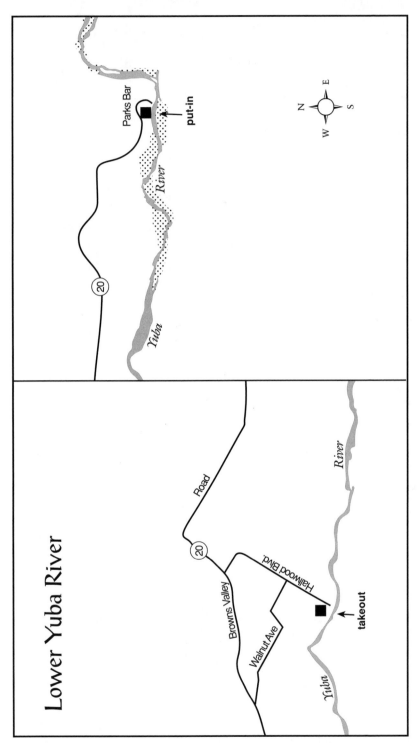

Paddling Area 2:
The Lower Yuba River

Trip Length: 14 miles

Maps: USGS Topographic Quadrants:
Smartville Quadrangle, 7.5 minute series
Browns Valley Quadrangle, 7.5 minute series
Yuba City Quadrangle, 7.5 minute series
USGS 1:250 000 scale map sections: Sacramento, Chico

Northern California Atlas and Gazetteer, DeLorme Mapping Co.,
1988, grid #78

Access: From Sacramento, take combined I-5 / State Highway 99
north for approximately seven miles. Exit onto combined state Highways 99 / 70 north (El Centro Road). After 13 miles, the highway
splits. Continue north on State Highway 70 for another 18 miles. This
highway eventually merges into State Highway 65. Continue on Highway 65 north for approximately 2.5 miles and exit on Feather River
Boulevard

Take Feather River Boulevard north for 1 block. Make a right turn
(south) onto North Beale Road. Continue on North Beale Road for 1
mile, then turn off onto Hammonton-Smartville Road going north.

After approximately 0.4 mile, merge left onto Simpson Lane (which becomes Ramirez Street at the Marysville city limits). Continue on until you reach State Highway 20. Turn right, take a deep breath, and congratulate yourself for not getting killed while reading these directions and driving at the same time!

You are now on the main road for the shuttle between your take-out and put-in. Continue on Highway 70 east for 3 miles, turn off onto Walnut Avenue (a right turn). Meander for another 2 miles until you reach the junction of Walnut Avenue and Hallwood Boulevard. Make a right turn onto Hallwood Boulevard, and follow it until it dead-ends at the bluff overlooking the Yuba River. Park without blocking either the driveway of the house on the left or the gate to the orchard on the right. (**Note:** Be sure to walk down to the river and familiarize yourself with the take-out, or you will be sight-seeing in Marysville and hitching a ride back to your car.)

To get to the put-in, take Hallwood Boulevard back to Highway 20. Turn right (east and continue for approximately 11 miles. Look for a turnoff to the right. You should see some houses there, just before crossing the new Yuba River bridge. Drive under the bridge and park on the shoulder of the old highway. The road nearest the river leads to a gravel pit, and gravel trucks use it on occasion. The launching site is on the west side of the bridge.

Difficulty: This stretch of the river, from the bridge to Marysville, is considered a Class I run, with a mandatory portage around the Daguerra Weir. The majority of obstacles encountered are either strainers or partially submerged rocks and other debris. If you are launching boats during a period of high water, be aware of the strong reverse eddy that may cause an upset if you aren't paying attention. On the open stretches of the river, particularly below the weir, strong afternoon headwinds are encountered.

I call this an "open" river, meaning that unlike so many of the Sierra rivers and their reservoirs enclosed in narrow canyons and gorges, the lower Yuba meanders through fairly gentle terrain that is surrounded by lush riparian vegetation (not counting the manmade cobble mounds left over from the gold dredges).

If you are fortunate enough to be boating during the salmon run, you may witness the truly spectacular sight of the fish fighting upstream to their spawning grounds. At the weir where you have to portage, be sure to take the time to view the fish ladder during the spawning season. Otherwise, the other point of historical interest is euphemistically listed on the topo maps as the Yuba Gold Fields. I call them "Great Big Piles of Rock." You will encounter these massive piles, some of which reach a height of over forty feet, at the toe of Long Bar, 1.5 river miles from the put-in.

Access to this area has generated considerable and heated debate by federal, state and local interests. In 1996 a law was passed allowing public use and travel through the area. However, the controlling private consortium refuses to relinquish control of these piles of rock. Hopefully wiser heads will prevail, and the public may be allowed to explore instead of further exploit this area of historical and environmental interest.

In summer, the residual heat from the exposed cobbles adds to the already uncomfortable air temperature. The turkey vultures use the rising heat currents emanating from the mounds for a "lift" as they cruise the river banks. On the plus side, the dredges that once operated here have left behind countless backwater channels and ponds just waiting to be explored. I have seen otters, beaver and countless species of birds when I have taken time to explore these areas. Another fun thing to do is to paddle into one of the side channels and see if it connects back to the river. Just be aware of the time so that you are not caught with miles to go before you sleep.

A sure sign of beaver

Just before the weir, large warning signs are posted on both sides of the river. The side channel for the portage is on river left. Follow the arrows to the end of the channel where you will then have to carry your boat up and over Daguerra Point. The portage ends at the south side of the weir, just below the fish ladder.

Take the time to scout the rock garden below the dam. You will have to negotiate a path with your boat. The river braids here into two channels. The best and easiest route is the main left channel. The last time I paddled here, I explored the far right channel and came upon a family of beavers swimming in the side ponds near the right bank.

The remaining stretch of river widens about 1/2 mile below the weir and loses its belt of riparian habitat. The cottonwoods, willows and oaks are replaced with walnut groves and other orchards. As the river erodes the banks holding the orchards, rows of walnut trees slide down into the river. If you are paddling during harvest season, usually in the fall, a quick eddy turn may reward you with a snack of ripe walnuts.

The sound and sight of gravel quarries become part of the scenery. Be ready to dodge the fishing lines cast out by increasing numbers of bank fishermen.

The first indication that your take-out is approaching are overhead power lines approximately two miles from the weir. The second indication is the sound of the gravel quarry. Finally, look for the walnut orchard on river right high on the bluff. With luck, you will spot your car as you paddle around the left bend and catch the eddy at the take-out on the cobble beach, just below the bluff where you parked your vehicle.

Other Sources:

Sutter and Yuba Counties, Compass Maps Inc., 1993 ed.

Notes

Grazing Mule Deer

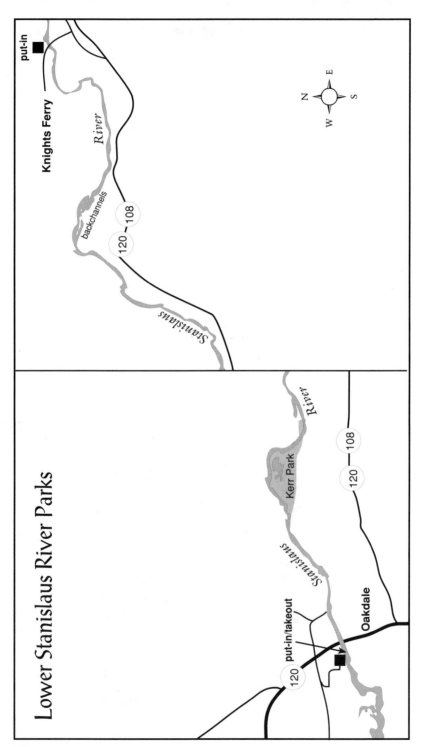

Lower Stanislaus River Parks

put-in

Knights Ferry

River

backchannels

120 — 108

Stanislaus

N
E
S
W

River

Kerr Park

108
120

Stanislaus

Oakdale

120

put-in/takeout

CHAPTER 6

The Sierra Foothills:
Southern Gold Fields
The Mother Lode Region

PADDLING AREA 1:
Lower Stanislaus River Parks

Trip Length: 14 miles

Maps: **USGS Topographical Quadrant:**
Knights Ferry Oakdale
USGS 1: 250,000 Scale: San Jose, CA

Northern California Atlas & Gazetteer, DeLorme Mapping Co.,
1988, grids #107 and #108

Access: From Sacramento, take I-5 or State Highway 99 south
through Stockton. Pick up road J9 or French Camp Road to Highway
120 east. Continue on 120 to Oakdale. At Oakdale, you can make the
decision about which section of the river to paddle.

Described here is the more popular run, from Knight's Ferry to
Oakdale Recreational Area down-river from the Highway 120 Bridge
(Oakdale / Waterford Highway) outside of Oakdale. The quickest
route to Knight's Ferry involves crossing the river and driving on
combined highways 108 and 120 east for approximately 13 miles.
Park in the visitor's center parking lot nearest the historic wooden
bridge over the river. This is your put-in.

If you have never been here before, be sure to visit the excellent
museum and visitor's center. The Army Corps of Engineers provides
free maps of the Stanislaus River Parkway and other boating and
recreational areas administered by the Corps.

Difficulty: From Knight's Ferry down to Durham Ferry State Recreation Area in "good ole San Joaquin City," this stretch of the Stanislaus River is a classic moving-water canoe paddle, and to make things interesting, this stretch does have a moderate Class II rapid, located about a half-mile below Knight's Ferry, known as "Russian Rapid." Just before the rapid, the river makes a sharp bend to the left and narrows to a slick clay bank on the right. Dense vegetation and the sharp bend make it difficult to spot the rapid.

The rapid itself is caused by a small hole below a ledge. The approach is on the left, which cannot be seen from up-river unless you stop and scout the rapid. If the rapid is too difficult to run, you can make a short portage on the river left.

Other hazards come from strainers (tree branches and other debris above and below the water line that may catch unwary boaters) and possible fence lines placed across the river by ranchers ignorant of the waterways law.

This section of the Stanislaus is a fine example of a riparian habitat teeming with birds and small mammals. The trees that predominate are Fremont cottonwoods, California sycamore, and various willows. At Horseshoe Road Recreation Area Campground you can see a large grove of sycamores that line the length of the camp on river right.

Be sure to take the time to explore some of the side channels and backwaters. These are the places beaver, river otters and herons find to their liking.

Although this may be described as a scenic river, it certainly is not a wilderness. You will pass many homes built along the river and see evidence of cattle throughout the trip. I found the majority of people I came across to be friendly and helpful. One local fisherman even took the time to show me a channel to a backwater area where a family of river otter were playing and grooming each other.

Approximately five miles from Knight's Ferry, you will paddle through an exposed outcrop of volcanic rock. During spring and early summer the air is filled with the aerobatics of swallows. The rough-textured surface of the exposed volcanic rock makes ideal nesting sites for the birds. Fall paddling provides an extra bonus in color changes of the deciduous trees and shrubs along the river banks.

As of this writing, there are three canoe/boat camping sites on this stretch of the parkway. I have camped on two of the three and found them primitive (they flood during the runoff) but clean and quiet.

Other Sources:

Stanislaus River Parks. U.S. Army Corps of Engineers, Feb. 1993

Stanislaus River Parks Boat-In Camping handout, Sacramento
    District brochure no. 360-1-1, U.S. Army Corps of Engineers,
    Sacramento District, Oct. 1992

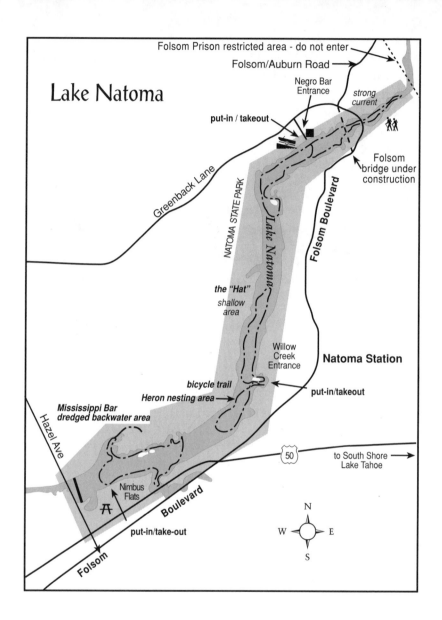

Lake Natoma

Folsom Prison restricted area - do not enter

Folsom/Auburn Road

Negro Bar Entrance

put-in / takeout

strong current

Greenback Lane

NATOMA STATE PARK

Lake Natoma

Folsom Boulevard

Folsom bridge under construction

the "Hat" shallow area

Willow Creek Entrance

Natoma Station

bicycle trail

Heron nesting area

put-in/takeout

Mississippi Bar dredged backwater area

Hazel Ave

50

to South Shore Lake Tahoe

Nimbus Flats

Boulevard

put-in/take-out

Folsom

N
W — E
S

94

CHAPTER 7

Sacramento Region: Highway 50 Corridor

Lake Natoma

Trip Length: Approximately 1/2 day. The lake has 13 miles of shore-line. Paddle length is determined by the put-in and destination of the paddler.

Maps: **USGS Topographical Quadrant:**
Folsom Quadrangle, 7.5 minute series

Access: The main entrance to the lake is located 16 miles east of downtown Sacramento off of U.S. Highway 50. Take the Hazel Avenue exit and you will see the lake as you cross over the freeway heading north. The main entrance is on your right adjacent to a commuter parking lot. Upon payment of fees, continue on the entrance road past the boat launch and park in the vehicle slots of the newly landscaped grassy beach and picnic area. From here it is a short walk to the lake and your launch site.

Additional launch areas on other parks of the lake are:

Willow Creek - an undeveloped use and boat launch site located 1/2 mile from the intersection of Folsom Boulevard and Blue Ravine Road. The entrance is off Auburn Road, but the road is one way so you must make a U-turn at the light on Blue Ravine Road.

Negro Bar - a popular family beach and paved boat launch with a floating dock. Located off Greenback Lane in Folsom.

Sacramento State University Aquatic Center - allows public access, but you must contact the facility for additional informa-tion and restrictions. Their phone number is 916-985-7739, and their fax number is 916-985-7312. The Aquatic Center is located at the entrance just north of Lake Natoma State Park.

Without a doubt, this is Sacramento's "multiple use and home-town lake." On any given weekend, it is common to see fishermen fishing in boats or on the banks, sailors sailing, students on sailboards, rowers rowing, and boaters boating in canoes, kayaks and everything in between. There is a 10 mph speed law on the east side of the lake, and a trolling-motor-only law on the west side.

Along the north shore, scores of bicyclists and skaters "burning the pavement" on the Jedediah Smith Bike Trail. (Skaters are allowed only on the portion of the bike trail running through state property.) Horseback riders exercising their mounts share parallel paths.

I think you've got the picture. This is definitely a high-impact area. However, I have also been on this same lake on an early summer morning with only a family of mallards to keep me company. Of all the places to choose from, for the purpose of paddling, I cannot imagine a friendlier location than Lake Natoma. If you are an aspiring boater practicing your skills or needing some exercise, then look no further.

Lake Natoma is the kind of place that, if a time restraint prevents a trip to a more wilderness setting, just a day or a few hours will satisfy that need to "get away."

The lake has three primary parks from which you can launch a boat and enjoy the beauty of the lake. These three entrances are also spread far enough apart to provide the paddler with different settings of the lake. The three state park entrances are:

(1) Lake Natoma Main Access (Nimbus Flats)
(2) Willow Springs
(3) Negro Bar Family Beach and Boat Launch

Great Blue Heron

PADDLING AREA 1:
Lake Natoma–Main Entrance,
Nimbus Flats Boat Launch

Access: The put-in is located at the main entrance, sometimes known as Nimbus Flats. To reach the park, take Highway 50 East to the Hazel Avenue exit. Cross over the highway going north, and make a right at the park entrance one-quarter mile from the highway exit.

Difficulty: This is the broadest and most windswept part of the lake. The prevailing wind is from the northwest (from the dam). Since this is a multi-use lake, you share the waters with a variety of water craft. In addition to the conventional boating scene, Lake Natoma hosts a healthy sculling crowd. Sacramento State University and the University of California at Davis sculling teams use the lake for practice. In late May and early June, two major rowing championships are held at the lake. Both races draw hundreds of spectators and the main part of the lake is closed to boating.

Recently a growing interest in the Polynesian style of racing and paddling outriggers has brought spectators for the annual outrigger races sponsored by Hui-O-Hawaii of Sacramento, the local Outrigger Canoe Club.

After a series of heavy rains, or in early spring, discharges from Folsom Dam and subsequently from Nimbus Dam take place for flood control purposes. These discharges generate a strong current carrying heavy debris through the lake. Check with the State Park Service before planning to paddle while these conditions are present.

During spring and summer, heavy drawdown of the lake's water for hydroelectric use occurs in the late evening. By morning, rock bars and other formerly submerged debris may become a hazard to boaters who are not used to paddling on the lake. These obstacles diminish with the rise of the lake during the course of the day.

Since the water entering Lake Natoma is released from the bottom of Folsom Lake, the water temperature is very cold (high 40s), even in the middle of summer. This is especially true at the upper part of the lake around Negro Bar.

This part of the lake is currently under major restoration and landscape design. As of this writing, the grassy picnic area and graded beach are the first step in a comprehensive master plan to redesign this section of the lake. You may choose to launch your boat in the small lagoon visible on the right as you enter the park. Or, if a barbecue or picnic is part of your plan, stake a claim to one of the picnic tables in the new grassy area and launch from the beach.

To enjoy this part of the lake and not be windblown or have to be constantly on the lookout for other boaters and swimmers, try paddling across the lake to the north shore. You will be rewarded with multiple small coves and bays that are fun to explore.

The scallop-shaped coves were formed by huge dredges scouring the shoreline for gold. Now they form deep holes that are home for fish and wildfowl. Furthermore, the coolness and clarity of the water make for a great swim. If you decide to paddle the lake in summer, by mid-July the blackberries are ripe and ready for picking.

After you finish exploring the coves, continue to paddle westward following the northern shoreline until you spot the bike and equestrian trail paralleling the lake shore. If you follow the bike trail with your boat, you will eventually come to a storm drain large enough to paddle through. Paddle underneath the bridge built on top of the drain and you will enter a part of Lake Natoma that only a few boaters and fishermen know.

This section of the lake was extensively dredged, leaving behind long stretches of waterway that created islands now heavily over-

Looking toward a heron rookery

Snowy egret

grown with tall, vine-covered sycamores. Deer browse and take shelter on these islands. It is not uncommon to come across a herd or an individual doe swimming from an island to the main shore. Families of acorn woodpeckers make their home in the dead snags standing on one of the islands. In the early morning or late afternoon, I have come across several beaver swimming in the ponds separating the islands.

When you return to the main part of the lake, follow the north shore line and paddle through the narrow channel that opens onto a familiar landmark on the lake. I'm referring to the exposed snags jutting out of the water close to the small island at the upper end of the channel. If you are fortunate, a small band of cormorants may be seen sunning themselves on the branches.

Farther up the lake, on the south shore next to the ranger's residence (the building visible from the lake), is the first "official" island sometimes known as "Ranger Rick Island." On a hot day the oak and pine trees growing on the island create a nice shady spot from which you can observe boats being paddled or sailed on the lake.

As you continue paddling farther up the lake, look for the tall digger pine trees growing on the edge of the bluffs. Some of them contain rope swings added by the locals. This activity is against the law and it is a constant battle between the park rangers cutting down the swings, and the local kids tying new ropes the next day.

Just before you reach the tall bluffs on the right side of the lake, look for concrete remnants of what used to be a pumping unit. Directly across on the other side of the lake, near a small brown rocky outcrop, is a bedrock mortar site. Adjacent to the bedrock mortars, approximately forty feet to the south, is a carved-out drainage canal built by miners operating the dredges before the construction of the lake.

Continue paddling on the north side of the lake and you will come to a small but private little beach just above the bedrock mortar site. This is a great spot to take a swim or view the towering bluffs on the south side of the lake.

If you are making this paddle during spring, bring a pair of binoculars and slowly drift by the stand of digger pines lining the north shore and surrounding the beach. Looking up, you will spot nests of the great blue heron within the branches of the trees. From personal experience, do not paddle directly underneath the nest sites; if the parent birds become stressed, their first reaction before flight is to void themselves—with you on the receiving end. In the late spring and early summer, snowy egrets will use the abandoned nests for their own nesting cycle.

Beyond the nesting trees is a string of buoys separating the lake from power boats. At this time you can either head back to the main beach, paddle into the small lagoon of Willow Creek, or continue up the lake to Negro Bar.

PADDLING AREA 2:
Lake Natoma–Willow Creek Access

Access: From the main entrance to Lake Natoma, take Hazel Avenue south. Cross over the freeway and make a left turn onto Folsom Boulevard (corner of Nimbus Winery shopping center). Proceed on Folsom Boulevard for approximately 2 miles. As you pass the Natoma outlet stores, Folsom Boulevard becomes a landscaped one-way road with no left turn access. Continue past the outlet center and make a U-turn at the intersection of Blue Ravine Road. Backtrack 1/2 mile and make a right turn at the Willow Creek Park entrance.

Difficulty: None. This sheltered lagoon is used by many of the local canoe and kayak schools to conduct their beginner classes. The only problem a novice paddler may encounter will be venturing onto the main lake from the sheltered lagoon. The winds may make it difficult to steer their boat in a straight line.

A small, tule-ringed lagoon protected from the winds blowing off the main lake provides the paddler with a friendly setting in which to launch a boat. As you paddle outward toward the lake, you will pass a small tree-covered island. If you paddle around the back side of the island, you will spot the eroded shapes of the different rocks that make up the bluffs on this part of the lake's shoreline. Upon entering the main lake, turn right and head for the island visible in the distance.

If you are not in any rush, paddle to the south shore and meander along the cobble-strewn beaches. Look for great blue herons among the cobbles as they hunt for frogs, mice and other delectable critters. As you cruise around the huge overhead point of dredge tailings, you will enter a small cove with an oak tree containing dead or leafless branches surrounded by blackberry bushes. The branches of the tree are used by the turkey vultures as perches from which to sun and preen themselves. For the last three years, I have spotted osprey perched on the bare limbs. Around late July, in the late afternoon when the water level is high enough to float up to the blackberry bushes, I bring a small pail and fill it with ripe berries.

At low water, an exposed cobble bar runs parallel with the north shore. It begins just beyond the tip of the large cobble mound that forms part of the shoreline, and continues past the island. It may cause you to scrape the underside of your boat if you're not paying attention.

Take time to visit the small island, known as "The Hat." It was originally a large pile of dredge tailings similar to the extensive mound visible on the northern horizon just as you enter the main lake from the lagoon. In the fall and winter months, Canada geese use the northern tip as a bedding site, probably because the elevated mound of cobbles provides a clear view of the lake and shields the geese from the prevailing wind.

Beyond the island, the lake widens before becoming narrow again at Negro Bar. This part of the lake becomes windblown during the afternoon. The next feature, a small back slough created by early dredging, is described in the next section. If you wish to paddle to Willow Springs or Nimbus Flats, use the right (north shore) side of the lake. The heavy vegetation with large cobble piles provides a nice windbreak.

Old Folsom Bridge

Paddling Area 3:
Lake Natoma–Negro Bar Boat Launch

Access: This part of the lake and park entrance is located within the city limits of Folsom. There are two primary routes to this section of the lake.

The first choice bypasses Willow Creek and makes the approach from the north. The second choice gives you the option of checking out the area of Willow Springs before continuing on to Negro Bar. Both routes average out about the same driving time.

Route 1: From the main entrance to Lake Natoma, make a right onto Hazel Avenue. Continue north on Hazel for approximately 2.5 miles. Make a right turn on Madison Avenue. Stay on Madison until it merges with Greenback Lane. As you merge onto Greenback Lane, you should see upper Lake Natoma on your right. Continue on Greenback Lane for approximately 1 mile and make another right at the entrance to Negro Bar.

Route 2: From the main entrance to Lake Natoma, make a left onto Hazel Avenue. Drive over State Highway 50. Make another left turn at the intersection of Hazel and Folsom Boulevard. Continue on Folsom for approximately 4.5 miles (soon after you enter the town of Folsom, Folsom becomes Sutter Street.) At the intersection of Sutter and Greenback Lane, merge onto Greenback. Cross over the historic Folsom Bridge and drive 1.3 miles to the Negro Bar entrance on your left.

Difficulty: None, unless paddled during heavy releases from Folsom Dam. When water is released from the larger dam, a strong current forms from Negro Bar up through the small gorge located up-river from Folsom Bridge. The current is not dangerous, but it can be difficult to paddle against on your return leg of the trip.

Since this part of Lake Natoma is so close to Folsom Dam, the water released from the dam has not had a chance to warm. The water temperature is too cold for swimming or prolonged immersion.

What can I say . . . this is my favorite part of the lake! When the lower lake is windblown, the bluffs and cobble mounds provide a windbreak allowing for an enjoyable paddle. The sandy main beach has public restrooms, a water fountain and picnic tables. During the summer, a lifeguard is on duty and a swimming area is designated by a string of buoys. If you do not own a boat yet, on Memorial Day weekend a rent-a-boat concession opens. A nominal fee is charged for boat rental. So if you wish to spend a day enjoying the water, I can't think of a better place than Negro Bar.

To enjoy some bird watching or spot a family of beaver, launch from the main beach and paddle directly to one of the inlets visible from the beach. The inlets lead into the dredged sloughs that are hidden by the cobble mounds. Exploring these channels, I have come across beaver, raccoon, and assorted waterfowl. In the deeper pools, you may spot fish swimming among the algae and water plants.

(**Note**: The best time to explore these back channels is at high water, usually in the late afternoon when the water level of the lake is high. However, at low water a sand bar becomes accessible on the island facing the bike trail, just at the bend of the lake. As the water level rises, this shallow area is warmed by the sun, providing a great place to swim.)

If you decide to paddle up the lake, stay along the south shore. Directly across from the boat launch visible on the opposite side, you will pass a shady spot that has a small beach and picnic table. Farther up, the lake begins to narrow and you begin to feel the tug of the current created by the water released from Folsom Dam.

If you make this paddle before construction of the new Folsom Bridge, take time to appreciate the view of the old bridge and the site of the rocky gorge beyond. When construction of the new bridge is complete, this classic view will be altered forever.

Just before you pass under the bridge, notice the old building on your right tucked under a grove of trees. This is the Folsom Powerhouse, site of the first transmission of long distance high voltage (for tours, phone: 916-988-0205). As you continue, the lake narrows considerably and you are within the narrow channel of the former South Fork of the American River. The current will continue to grow stronger as you make your way up the channel. In the summer, you will catch kids jumping and diving off the bridge and high rocky points within the gorge. Should you fight your way up the gorge, you will have to turn back upon encountering the large sign warning that you are entering a no-trespassing area controlled by Folsom State Prison.

Your return should be a lot easier with the current pushing your boat and giving you a chance to enjoy the scenery you missed in your upstream struggle.

Other Sources:

The American River Parkway, Jedediah Smith Memorial Trail,
The American River Parkway Foundation, 1995

Welcome to Your Parkway: Schedule and Guide to Use of the American River Parkway, The American River Parkway Foundation

A Boating Trail Guide to the American River Parkway, Sacramento County Department of Parks and Recreation & California Department of Boating and Waterways, Safety Hints and Guide Map

Recreational Lakes of California, by Dirksen & Reeves, Recreation Sales Publishing, 1996

Guidebook:

Sacramento's Outdoor World, A Local Field Guide, 1986 ed., American River Natural History Association / Sacramento County Office of Education, Sacramento County Parks, Effie Yeaw Nature Center

snowy egret

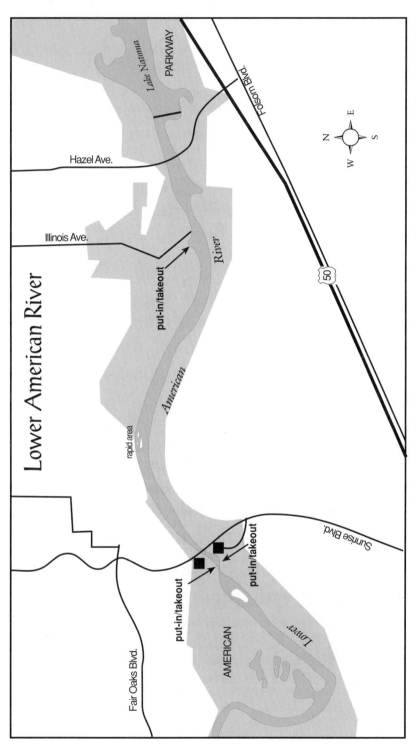

Lower American River

CHAPTER 8

Sacramento Region: Highway 50 Corridor– Lower American River Parkway

PADDLING AREA 1: Sailor Bar to Jims Bridge– Lower Sunrise / Sacramento Bar Accesses

Trip Length: 2.0 miles (approximately 1 hour paddling time)

Maps: **USGS Topographical Quadrants:**
Folsom Quadrangle, 7.5 minute series
Citrus Heights Quadrangle, 7.5 minute series
Carmichael Quadrangle, 7.5 minute series

Access: The put-in location is at the parkway facility of Sailor Bar, located off of Illinois Avenue. You reach it by taking Highway 50 east and exiting onto Hazel Avenue (the same exit as the one for the main entrance to Lake Natoma). Continue on Hazel Avenue crossing over Nimbus Dam. Make a left turn onto Winding Way (the second stop-

light after crossing the dam). Drive for approximately 1 mile and make a left turn onto Illinois Avenue. You will enter the American River Parkway approximately 1/2 mile from the turnoff. After paying the entrance fee, angle left on the gravel road and follow it to the cobbled parking area adjacent to the small pond near the river. **(Note:** Secure all valuables in the trunk or hide them from view. Because of their remote locations, all river parking areas are subject to vandalism and theft.)

The take-out at Jim's Bridge may be accessed from two parkway locations. The first and most common one is at the Lower Sunrise Parkway entrance on the south side of the river. The second access is at Sacramento Bar on the north side of the river.

Both locations are off Sunrise Boulevard, a major exit from Highway 50. From Sacramento, take State Highway 50 east. Exit onto Sunrise Boulevard and head north for approximately two miles. Make a right turn onto Bridge Street (the last turnoff before crossing the American River Bridge). Continue on Bridge Street to the parkway entrance station. Upon paying the fee, follow the road and make a left at the bottom of the small hill. Drive under the Sunrise Boulevard bridge ramp and park in the parking area near the small bridge known as Jim's Bridge. The take-out is at the small beach on the downriver side of the bridge.

To reach the Sacramento Bar access, instead of turning off onto Bridge street, continue on Sunrise Boulevard cross over the river and make the first left turn (Fair Oaks Boulevard) Make a second left onto Pennsylvania Avenue (one-tenth of a mile from the Sunrise-Fair Oaks intersection). Follow Pennsylvania Avenue down to the kiosk or entrance station. The take-out is the cobble beach on the downriver side of Jim's Bridge, a short walk from the parking area.

Difficulty: Although the entire section of the Lower American River is considered Class I, the combination of cold water, swift current and brushy banks requires basic boat-handling skills for a safe and enjoyable paddle. This section of the river has only one area that requires some attention by novice boaters: a series of strainers on river right in the center of a narrow left bend adjacent to an island at the Olive Avenue access.

This first section of the Lower American River is seldom paddled because it is easier just to access the Sunrise / Sacramento Bar sections and shorten the shuttle. However, some of the grandest views of the river and the Old Fair Oaks Bridge are to be experienced when paddling this short but lively stretch of river.

The small pond where you first put-in is a manmade backwater that floated a dredge named the "Hercules." This massive dredge was able to clear a path of two hundred feet wide and remove approximately 89,600 cubic feet of topsoil every 24 hours of a run. The remains of this ghastly operation is now visible from the mounds of cobbles stretching along both sides of the river. (For a better understanding of the size and mass of these dredges, see the photographs on pages 47–49 in *Gold Districts of California,* Bulletin 193; California Division of Mines and Geology and *Fair Oaks . . . The Early Years;* Fair Oaks Historical Society, pp. 18–19.) In the spring and summer, different kayak schools use this pond to introduce their students to the introductory skills of whitewater kayaking. You will see students practicing the Eskimo roll and proper paddling strokes before they venture onto the flowing river.

Twice a year, once in June and once in August, this spot becomes crowded with boats and boaters participating in the River City Marathon Race starting at Sailor Bar and ending 17 miles downriver at Paradise Beach near the Sacramento State University campus. In August, participants prepare their boats for the shorter Gristmill Race, a fast-paced 10.5 paddle to the Gristmill Access. Both races are sponsored by River City Paddlers, a local paddling club in Sacramento.

At other times the pond sits quiet, and only the ripples of ducks feeding along the banks mar the stillness of the water. Look for turtles sunning themselves on the northeast corner of the pond. If you are quiet long enough, the deep sound of a bullfrog may resound from the shadows formed by the bushes along the bank.

The pond provides a leisurely chance to warm up and stretch your muscles for the paddle ahead. In the heat of summer, the waters are deep and cool enough to dive and swim in, unlike the cold, swift waters of the river.

When you are ready, use the eddy line that forms at the mouth of the pond to position your bow downstream and into the main current. Stay away from the shallow area alongside the cobble bar that juts out on your left as you enter the river. Stay to river right and you will be in the deeper main channel where your paddle won't strike against any rocks.

As you drift downriver, look back and enjoy the view of the river as it sweeps around Sailor Bar. Directly across the river on the upper bank is the Jedediah Smith Memorial Bike Trail which begins in Old Town, Sacramento, follows the American River to the Nimbus Fish Hatchery, parallels Lake Natoma, and terminates at Folsom Lake.

As you pass small clumps of brush and vegetation on river right, watch for herons standing silently as they wait for their prey to pass within striking distance of their stiletto-like beaks. Small clusters of Canada geese and mergansers sometimes feed in the small eddies that form in the scalloped banks along the river. Keep a sharp eye peeled for fishermen who, not expecting a boat to float past them, cast their lines into the middle of the channel.

Approximately 800 yards downriver on river right you will pass a standing snag. Look for the belted kingfisher that sits on the limb of the deadwood. The small cavities in the trunk are often times used as nests by other birds. Sometimes the limbs of this snag act as a perch for the turkey vulture. The presence of vultures is common in late fall when the salmon begin their migration up the river.

As the river straightens, on river right are many clusters of oaks. During the fall and winter months, you may spot acorn woodpeckers as they carry acorns to their hiding places among the oak trees.

There are many small backwaters created by dredges that are fun to eddy into and explore. One backwater is located on river left just before the river begins its bend to the left. At the far end of the pond is a pile of branches and brush signifying a beaver lodge. Hidden in the brush are entrances to tunnels dug into the mudbank, providing an escape route for the beaver.

When you are ready to proceed, take time to decide which route you feel most comfortable with. Looking down river, you will notice that the river splits into two channels as it braids around the small island in the center of the river. The channel on river right is the most difficult of the two. If the flow is at 2,000 cfs (cubic feet per second) or greater, you should spot the tell-tale frothy heads of a series of standing waves (the wonderfully descriptive "White Horses" of Sigurd F. Olson's *The Lonely Land*) in the center of the channel. The left bend of the river forces the current to sweep the right bank containing a series of strainers (downed trees). Left of the standing waves, the river passes over a shallow cobble bar that would hang a canoe or kayak on the rocks. To negotiate this stretch, you must be prepared to brace against the churning water created by the "White Horses," then cross-ferry around the strainers.

The second channel consists of a series of riffles and a slight bank to the right around the island.

The "fly in the ointment" to this second approach has to do with the amount of flow. Anything below 1,500 cfs makes this second channel too shallow to negotiate. **(Note:** At flows above 2,100 cfs, the water level washes out most of the strainers, allowing for a less technical run. The left channel becomes swifter and deeper with an unobstructed passage. The right channel still has the standing waves and churning water to contend with.)

When the thrill is gone, you will settle onto the broadened stretch of the river with its grand view downriver of the old Fair Oaks bridge. The steep high banks on river right are locally called "The Bluffs." Their ownership is currently under dispute between local property owners and Sacramento County. The views from these bluffs is indeed magnificent, but until the dispute is resolved, access to them is restricted.

Riffles ahead . . .

To your immediate left is the Upper Sunrise access with its small concrete boat launch and somewhat sandy beach.

As you get closer to the old bridge, be wary of the concrete abutments. The strength of the current is deceptive due to the wide, deep channel. It takes only a moment for your boat to broach against the concrete and become pinned by the pressure of the moving water.

Once you have passed the old bridge, if you are taking out at Lower Sunrise, paddle toward river left and clear the buoy marking an obstacle in the channel. The second overpass you paddle under is Sunrise Boulevard, and then you should spot the smaller abutments belonging to Jim's Bridge. (The original bridge was built by a local gravel company to move cobbles from Sacramento Bar on the north side to their operations area at Lower Sunrise. When the area came under county control, the bridge was named for Jim Jones, who played an important role in the creation of the American River Parkway). As you make your approach to the beach immediately past the bridge, be extremely wary of the current as it sweeps around the abutments.

For those of you who parked at Sacramento Bar, to avoid scraping your boat or paddles in the shallows, start a gradual approach to beach your boat on the cobble bar before Jim's Bridge, or carefully negotiate the bridge and ferry out into the eddy on the downriver side of the bridge.

If you haven't already noticed, there are clean cinder block restrooms and drinking fountains available at both access points.

Other Sources:

The American River Parkway, Jedediah Smith Memorial Trail, The American River Parkway Foundation, 1995

Welcome to your Parkway: Schedule and Guide to the use of the American River Parkway, The American River Parkway Foundation

A Boating Trail Guide to the American River Parkway, Safety Hints and Guide Map, Sacramento County Department of Parks & Recreation / California Department of Boating and Waterways, 1993 ed.

Guidebook:

Sacramento's Outdoor World, A local Field Guide, American River Natural History Association, Sacramento County Office of Education, Sacramento County Parks, Effie Yeaw Nature Center, 1986 ed.

Notes

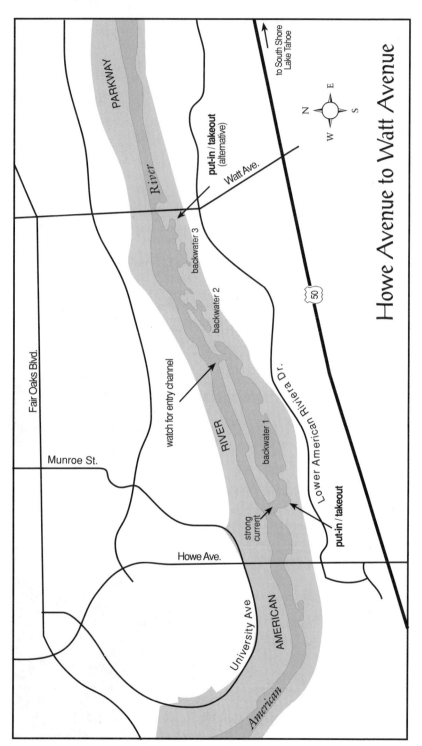

Howe Avenue to Watt Avenue

114

PADDLING AREA 2:
Howe Avenue Access to Watt Avenue Access

Trip Length: Approximately 1.5 miles one way
(paddling time will vary)

Maps: USGS Topographical Quadrants
Sacramento East, 7.5 minute series

Access: If a shuttle is available, it would make sense to put in at Watt
Avenue and take out at Howe Avenue (Howe being downriver from
Watt). If a shuttle isn't available, or you just wish to explore and not
restrict yourself to the flow of the river, put in and take out at Howe
Avenue. I'd rather paddle up the river when I'm fresh and spry and
then float back down when I'm hot and tired. With this bit of logic in
mind, your route from Sacramento to Howe Avenue would entail
taking State Highway 50 east and turning off at the Power-Inn / Howe
Avenue exit. Turn north over the freeway and make a right exit for La
Riviera Drive, located only a short distance from the highway
overcrossing. Cross over La Riviera Drive into the entrance for Howe
Avenue Parkway. Upon payment of the fee, park closest to the stand
of cottonwoods located at the far end of the parking lot. Your destination is the large lagoon-like backwater paralleling the river.

If a shuttle is planned, drive out the entrance and make a left turn onto La Riviera Drive. Continue on La Riviera for approximately 1.5 miles. When you drive under the Watt Avenue overpass, you will pass by the Watt Avenue Access. Make a U-turn at the stoplight and enter the Watt Avenue Parkway entrance. Drive over the levee and park under the Watt Avenue overpass. Your put-in is a small back-water on the immediate downriver side of the nearest abutment facing the river.

An alternative to using La Rivera Drive is to take Highway 50 east to the Watt Avenue exit approximately 1.2 miles east of Howe Avenue. Upon exiting from the highway, head north over the freeway, exit right (just before crossing the Watt Avenue bridge) at the small sign stating River Access. Make a left at the light (La Riviera Drive) and an immediate right into the parkway entrance.

Difficulty: This is a flat-water paddle with no rapids or technical maneuvers. You will be using the river current to access the lagoons and return to your vehicles. The primary consideration should be the flow of the American River. A normal flow is between 1500 to 2500 cfs.

For up-to-date flow information on the American and other rivers, call K-Flow at 916-368-8682, or the Sacramento County of Parks & Recreation at 916-366-2072 for the flow on the Lower American River.

For clarification, this paddle is described as originating and taking out at Howe Avenue.

Here's a paddle that provides you with a chance to experience nature, get some exercise or take the family on an outing without having to drive for miles. If you are a solo paddler, and anxious to "get a feel for the river" but have no way to shuttle your boat, then this paddle is made for you.

Put in at the far end of Howe Avenue parking lot, just below the narrow drive-around located next to a small group of tall cotton-woods. Try to launch your boat as close to the upper far right bank as you can; otherwise, the pull of the current will push you into the river's main channel.

If you look up-river, you will notice that the large sandy island acts as a barrier between the flowing river and the large backwater in which you will be paddling. At the far upstream end of the island there is an opening where the river enters and separates the island from the main shore. This finger of land is also separated by a wide but narrow backwater that dead-ends into the trees and brush of the upper shore. Prior to the flood of 1986, this area was indeed a large lagoon separated from the river by a barrier of land stretching from Howe Avenue to where the power lines cross the river, approximately 1/2 mile upstream.

The best time to make this paddle is either in the early morning, late afternoon, or on a calm overcast or even drizzly day. These are prime conditions to spot the many animals that live in and around the river. As you begin the paddle, look in the bushes along the shore on your right. Often I have flushed river otters, herons and even deer that were feeding along the bank. Stay to the right bank as you initially paddle from the put-in and you won't be fighting the current.

When you pass the upper opening to the river, aim for the small backwater to the far right of the bank facing the river. If you are making this paddle in the early morning or in the late afternoon, make your approach slowly and quietly. Many times I have spotted great blue herons fishing in the shallows of the upper end of this backwater. Sometimes you can see river otters swimming and diving for fish among the fallen limbs along the banks.

When you are ready to proceed, paddle through the opening that separates this backwater from the river and, staying in the eddies along the right shoreline, make your way up-river into the next backwater.

You will recognize the narrow entrance because of the high sandy embankment at the left end of the opening. This beach is a good spot to take a break before proceeding. Depending on the time of year, the cavities in the large snag facing the river are used as nests by different bird species; I have spotted acorn woodpeckers, red shafted flickers and an owl.

Before you enter this small backwater, scan the edges of the shore for limbs or other objects sticking out of the water. Many times turtles like to bask on these convenient "plopping spots" (at the first hint of strange sounds or movement, the turtles "plop" into the water).

Sacramento is home to the western pond turtle. If you are stealthy, you may be rewarded with a sighting of one or more of these shy reptiles as they warm themselves near the water.

The last backwater you will enter is visible from the previous backwater.

During periods of high water, often in the winter and early spring, all these back channels become flooded and are interconnected. Prior

Flood debris in first backwater

to the taming of the river by the building of Folsom Dam, these back channels would appear and disappear depending on the sediment deposited during flooding. Now, however, many of these small lagoons have become almost a permanent part of the river.

The vegetation covering the banks of this last area of backwater is often times mistaken for bamboo. The giant reed is a close relative of bamboo, but the tall stalks are more brittle than bamboo. These large clumps of reed provide a hiding place for many small rodents and other animals. I have spotted raccoons and skunks darting into the undergrowth of the reed plants.

The cleared cobble bar up-river from the stand of reeds marks the Watt Avenue access. The parking area is located directly below the overpass and a rest room with a public telephone sits on the edge of the levee approximately 100 yards below the overpass.

If you are planning to return to Howe Avenue, paddle downstream staying to river left. **(Note:** Make sure that you don't miss the downstream opening that was first used to enter the river from the backwater at Howe Avenue. The strong sweep of the current below the island at Howe Avenue makes it difficult to eddy into the quiet waters of the backwater near your take-out.)

Upon entering the backwater where you were paddling earlier, if you want to explore the island that separates this area from the river, now is the time to do so. When you are ready to return to the lagoon, paddle hard to avoid being caught by the downstream current sweeping past the island.

Upon returning to the Howe Avenue access, beach your boat to the left of the boat launch so that others may launch their craft while you unload.

Other Sources:

The American River Parkway, Jedediah Smith Memorial Trail, The American River Parkway Foundation, 1995

Welcome to Your Parkway: Schedule and Guide to the Use of the American River Parkway, The American River Parkway Foundation

A Boating Trail Guide to the American River Parkway, Safety Hints and Guide Map, Sacramento County Department of Parks & Waterways, 1993 ed.

Guidebook:

Sacramento's Outdoor World, A Local Field Guide, American River Natural History Association, Sacramento County Office of Education, Sacramento County Parks, Effie Yeaw Nature Center, 1986 ed.

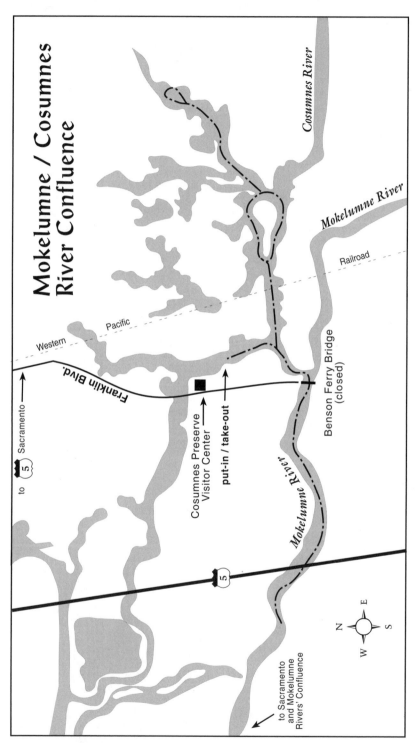

Mokelumne / Cosumnes
River Confluence

Cosumnes River

Mokelumne River

Railroad

Western   Pacific

Franklin Blvd.

to Sacramento

to ⑤ 5

Cosumnes Preserve
Visitor Center

put-in / take-out

Benson Ferry Bridge
(closed)

Mokelumne River

⑤ 5

N
W   E
S

to Sacramento
and Mokelumne
Rivers' Confluence

CHAPTER 9

Sacramento Region: Delta Country– Highway 95 & I-5 Corridors

PADDLING AREA 1: Mokelumne, Cosumnes River Confluence & Back Sloughs

Trip Length: Approximately 4.5 miles round trip

Maps: **USGS Topographic Quadrants:**
Bruceville Quadrant, 7.5 minute series
Galt Quadrant, 7.5 minute series
USGS 1:250 000 Scale: Sacramento, CA

Northern California Atlas and Gazetteer, Delorme Mapping Co. 1988, grid #96, section B-3

The Thomas Guide Series, Sacramento County, 1996, maps #417 and 418

Peace and quiet

Access: From Sacramento, take I-5 South, or, for a slower but more interesting route, take county route J8, better known as Franklin Boulevard. If coming off the interstate, exit at Twin Cities Road (E13). Continue east on Twin Cities Road for approximately 1.5 miles. At the junction of Twin Cities Road and Franklin, turn right onto Franklin. **Note:** At the time of this writing, due to the 1997 flooding, the Benson Ferry Bridge is closed to all but local traffic. Therefore, access to the road that leads to the original put-in is not available. The new launch site is reached as you continue south on Franklin Boulevard for approximately 2.5 miles. You pass the Cosumnes Preserve Visitor Center on your left. Pull over immediately onto a shoulder on driver's left upon crossing the first bridge past the visitor's center. Below the road bed is a slough and a flood plain. This is a back slough of the Cosumnes River and your access to the main Cosumnes River, the Mokelumne River, and a system of sloughs.

Difficulty: Although this is quiet-water paddling at its best, four noteworthy points should be taken into account to make the paddle an enjoyable experience.

First, unlike lakes or reservoirs, sloughs are subject to the rise and ebb of the tide. Before venturing out to paddle on the sloughs, check the tidal guide for the time and height of the tides in the area to be paddled. Getting caught in a slough during slack or low tide means wading through deep boot-sucking mud or waiting (for up to three hours) for enough water to float the boats before further paddling can be done.

Second, be sure you are familiar with the paddling area and that you have a map to aid you with your route-making (at present there are no maps that are current or reliable, but what exists is better than nothing). Unless you or one of the other paddlers have experience paddling in a slough, the channels all begin to look alike. Getting lost takes on a whole new meaning.

Third, when paddling in the spring or early summer, take plenty of insect repellent and your own secret bug juice, eat garlic or use any other precautions to protect you from the hordes of mosquitoes and other insects determined to have you for their lunch.

Fourth, carry and drink plenty of water. Because of the heavy vegetation cover, very little wind makes its way into some of the sloughs, and the air becomes humid and dense. This condition may rapidly cause the paddler to become dehydrated. Only generous amounts of liquid (beer does not count) remedy this situation.

If animal and bird viewing are your interests, then this paddle is for you! The best time of year is either spring or fall.

When exploring the many backwaters and muddy beaches on this leg of the river, I recommend rubber boots, or the leather-toe / rubber-bottom Maine hunting shoe. You will be climbing in and out of the boat as you portage over the brush and debris piles formed during the spring floods and now slick with mud and algae. Wear a hat with a wide brim for both sun and chance of showers, and loose clothing to protect against brush and bugs. If you are into the flora

Train crossing Cosumnes River Slough

A good fishing spot

and fauna, a pair of binoculars, a camera with a telephoto lens, and a guidebook are necessities.

As mentioned earlier, all the sloughs to be explored in this area are entered on the left off the small channel of the Cosumnes River. The pathway to the water is on the south side of the bridge leading onto the flood plain. If you are launching at low tide, be careful of the slick muddy banks. Upon launching, you will notice a small channel directly across from where you launched. This is the channel that leads to the Cosumnes Preserve. The main slough, however, is on your right and begins to widen as you paddle past the tule beds.

Continue to paddle until you reach a confluence. You are now on the Cosumnes River. Looking down the Cosumnes you can spot the steel train trestle that belonged to the Western Pacific railroad. At different times of the day you will feel a deep rumble and hear the air horn of the approaching train. My friend Todd and I like to paddle under the trestle as the train goes by to feel the power of the train and hear the noise of its passing.

Continuing down the river past the trestle, check the debris cached against the pilings. I have found duck, goose, and even turkey decoys partially exposed in the debris. Beyond the trestle you come to a fork in the river. The Cosumnes River flows to the right and the main sloughs are to your left. There are several side bays and channels that promise lots of ducks, herons and egrets. Be sure to check the tules for the elusive green-backed heron and the pie-billed grebe. If you are fortunate, you'll spot a marsh hawk in the act of catching its dinner. As you continue with the paddle, stay close to the bank and you may spot turtles sunning themselves on the exposed branches or logs on the water's surface. Look for undercut mud banks that may hide river otters preening themselves. A V-wake on the surface of the water could be the head of a beaver, muskrat, or otter.

If you turn right at the confluence and paddle for approximately 400 yards around the small bend, you reach the main confluence of the Cosumnes and Mokelumne rivers. Making a left or right turn here places you on the Mokelumne River. You should be able to tell that you have entered the Mokelumne River by the clarity of the water. While the waters of the Cosumnes flow a dirty, silt-laden brown, the Mokelumne is clearer and colder.

On your right or down-river, you will spot the concrete abutments of the Benson Ferry Bridge. Look carefully at the bridge and note the huge gearing that allowed the bridge to pivot when a tall boat needed to pass underneath. During the late spring and early summer, the bridge acts as a nesting site for another marvelous "engineer," namely, the cliff swallow. As you paddle under the bridge, the air is alive with hundreds of darting birds carrying either mud for the multitude of nests situated along the underside of the bridge, or food to their nestlings.

If you choose to continue, you pass under the I-5 overpass and eventually reach New Hope Landing approximately 10 miles down-river. From there, you may continue on until you reach the confluence of the Mokelumne with the Sacramento River below Brannan Island.

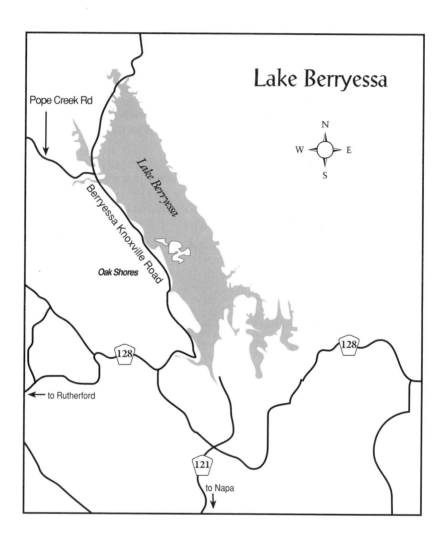

Lake Berryessa

Pope Creek Rd

Lake Berryessa

Berryessa Knoxville Road

Oak Shores

128

128

← to Rutherford

121

to Napa

CHAPTER 10

The North Coast Ranges: I-80 Corridor

PADDLING AREA 1:
Lake Berryessa, Oak Shores Park, The Islands

Trip Length: 1/2 day or longer

Maps: USGS Topographic Quadrants:
Lake Berryessa, 7.5 minute series
Chiles Valley, 7.5 minute series
Walter Springs, 7.5 minute series

Northern California Atlas & Gazetteer, DeLorme Map Co., 1996 ed.

Access: From Sacramento, take I-80 west. Exit north onto State Highway 113. Drive 3 miles and exit, heading west, onto County road E6 (West Covell Boulevard). When you pass through the town

of Winters, E6 becomes State Route 128. Continue on route 128 west for approximately 22 miles. At the State Routes 121 / 128 junction, turn right, staying on route 128. Drive 5 miles and turn right on Knoxville Road. After 6.5 miles, you will see the sign on your right, marking the entrance to the visitor's center.

The Oak Shores Park entrance, again on the right, is approximately 1/2 mile further down the road. The put-in for Pope Canyon is approximately 6 miles from the visitor's center. Look for a large gravel parking area on the left immediately after crossing the Pope Canyon Bridge (the first bridge).

Difficulty: This is a classic flatwater paddle. When the wind is gusting on the outer lake, the islands act as a wind block, allowing the paddler to comfortably explore them. Although buoys posting a speed limit are evident, some of the "cowboys" in boats use the island waterways as a shortcut to the main lake.

Your greatest problem, however, will be to remember the inlet you started from so that when it comes time to return, the words "oh-oh" won't be on your lips.

"Lake Berryessa for paddling? Be serious!" I am serious. The notoriety associated with Lake Berryessa is limited to the late spring and summer months; therefore, I paddle the lake in the spring and fall. Not only are the hordes of motorboaters, water skiers, and jet skiers gone, but the air temperature is better suited for paddling. By late spring, the green grasses of the surrounding foothills begin to dry out and turn brown. The delicate wildflowers wilt and die off in the increasing heat. The majority of migrating birds such as the common loon, western grebe, Canada goose and other bird visitors become scarce with the approach of summer, but the crowds and competition for parking, camping and water use *increase.*

By applying some judicious timing, you will be able to enjoy the lake in a canoe or kayak. Because the size of Lake Berryessa makes canoeing and kayaking a difficult sport to enjoy as an afternoon or day venture, I limit my description to two areas that will give you a "feel for the lake."

The first area is situated offshore from the only major public access to Lake Berryessa, namely Oak Shores Park. In the second location, you can experience boating in an inlet that gradually narrows and eventually becomes Pope Creek, a secondary source for Lake Berryessa.

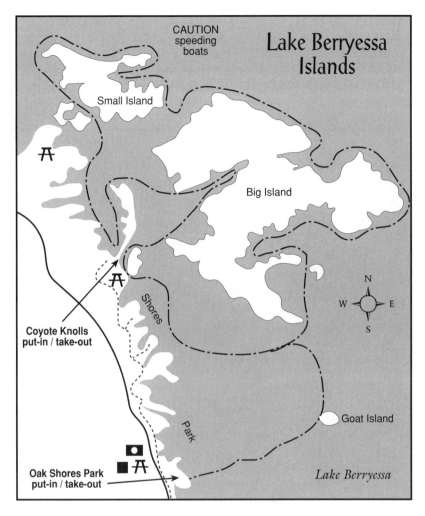

The map shows Lake Berryessa Islands with the following labels:

CAUTION speeding boats

Lake Berryessa Islands

Small Island

Big Island

Shores

Park

Coyote Knolls put-in / take-out

Goat Island

Oak Shores Park put-in / take-out

Lake Berryessa

N W E S

The Islands

Access: The best location for put-in to paddle the islands is Oak Shores Park. If you feel that trying to remember which inlet you launched from may be a problem, use any of the sites south of the park's entrance station. Otherwise, park at Coyote Knolls and launch from any of the sites closest to your parking spot. (**Note:** Due to the narrow dimensions of the park, the road inside the park is one-way. If you pass by or hesitate in your decision, be prepared to exit the park and return. Also, the entrance to Coyote Knolls—north side— requires a partial loop to the left after you pass the kiosk, otherwise you may be committed to sightseeing the beaches and picnic areas on the south side of the park.)

If you use the lake in the off season, an additional benefit is free parking at some of the facilities such as Oak Shores Park. Beginning in late spring, there is a day use fee. For information on fees and other questions, contact the ranger by phone: 707-966-2111, fax: 707-966-0409, or e-mail: ldickey@2bro100.vip.usbr.gov.

Oak Shores take-out

If you really want to appreciate this paddle, then make every effort to be on the water as early as you can; sunrise is ideal. The glassy calm of the water and the thrill of hearing a loon call as the sun warms your face is worth the effort it took you to make the drive. As you leave the shoreline behind, the first island looms in the foreground. If you have launched from any of the beaches south of the entrance station, the lone island you see in the distance is Goat Island. When the island's details are clearly discerned, you will notice that the lone snag standing sentinel holds a large osprey nest. With luck, one or both parent birds are on or near the nest. Although no signs are posted, please refrain from beaching and hiking to the nest tree. I usually paddle to a group of trees on the left (north) side that hide me, yet still allow a clear view of the nest.

From Goat Island you can explore the other islands, starting with Big Island, located to the north of Goat Island. By planning your paddle in a counterclockwise direction, you will get a chance to explore the outer coastline of the islands before the wind picks up. The windy afternoon will find you enjoying island scenery, screened from the full wind gusts and choppy waters of the main lake.

Cross the main channel separating Big Island from Small Island and pop into the easterly cove of Small Island. This is a nice break spot where you may see deer and Canada geese browsing along the oak-covered shore.

Heading out, watch for speeding bass boats as you round the northern finger of Small Island. Follow the shoreline, and you will

Goat Island

spot the Lake Berryessa Marina / Resort. Here is your entrance into the islands that make up the rest of Oak Shores Park, and the remainder of your paddle. When paddling amongst the smaller islands, remember that the through-channel back to your take-out is on your left (east), and that you will pass by the west side of Big Island before you sight your beach.

Among the islands

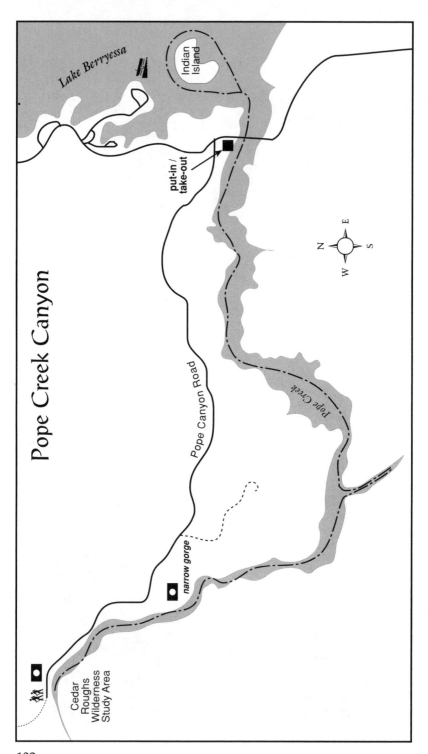

Pope Creek Canyon

Lake Berryessa

Indian Island

put-in / take-out

Pope Canyon Road

Pope Creek

narrow gorge

Cedar Roughs Wilderness Study Area

N E W S

Paddling Area 2: Pope Creek Canyon

Access: For the best launching area, continue past Oak Shores Park and cross over the Pope Creek Bridge. Make a left turn onto Pope Canyon Road, and another left into the large gravel parking lot overlooking Pope Creek Channel. Try to park near the bridge because the trail down to the water is located near the bridge abutment closest to the parking lot. Follow the trail down and launch from the beach underneath the bridge.

Before you begin paddling up the channel, take a moment to paddle around Indian Island, located on the left just outside the

Pope Creek Canyon from Pope Creek Bridge

mouth of the channel. As you head back from the island, upon passing underneath the bridge, stay to the right and close to the rock walls of the canyon. In early spring, clusters of succulents with red stems and yellow globular heads grow out of the many crevices in the canyons walls.

The channel eventually makes a bend to the left and broadens into a wide bay. Stay to the right and be prepared for the wind gusts on your left (port) side. In the spring or early summer, the hills surrounding the bay provide a nice contrast of green against the blue waters of the open bay. The steep slopes on the southwest side generate thermals that provide lift for the turkey vultures seen circling the pines, oaks and manzanita that grow to the water's edge.

By paddling alongside the right (north) bank, you will have access to the beaches that are created by the gentle slope of the hills. Eventually the channel narrows and you paddle past the steep canyon walls that gradually become part of Pope Creek.

Depending on the time of year, if the water level is high you might have to paddle through the flooded brush that hides the flowing waters of the creek. Once past the brushy wall, beach your boat and explore the creek bed. If the weather cooperates and it is a warm spring day, you may enjoy a swim in one of the deep pools of the creek.

As you make your way up the creek bed, you enter the 6,500 acre Cedar Roughs Wilderness Study Area. The ridges above Pope Creek Canyon contain the world's largest stand of genetically-pure Sargent cypress. Hiking the streambed, you will notice a greenish rock that appears to have a slick appearance and feels soapy or greasy to the touch. This rather curious rock is serpentine and has the honor of being our official state rock.

Paddling back, stay along the right (south) shore and you will be able to glimpse small groups of deer as they have their evening drink before browsing. Families of Canada geese hide in the shadows along with mergansers and other ducks. Eventually you will spot the bridge and the beach where you launched your boat.

Other Sources:

Clear Lake / Lake Berryessa, Fish-n-Map Co. Inc.

Lake Berryessa, FHS Maps, Map #A-126, 1995

Lake Berryessa, U.S. Dept. of the Interior, Bureau of Reclamation handout

Oak Shores Park, Bureau of Reclamation handout

Notes

Appendix 1

Maps and Navigation

USGS (United States Geological Survey)Topographical Maps
[7.5 Minute Map Sheets, 1: 24 000 Scale]

The American River, North Fork: *Colfax, Greenwood*

The American River below Folsom Dam: *Folsom, Carmichael, Sacramento East*

Lake Spaulding: *Blue Canyon, Cisco Grove*

Lake Valley Reservoir: *Cisco Grove*

Lake Clementine: *Auburn, Greenwood*

Folsom Lake (North Arm): *Pilot Hill, Rocklin, Folsom*

Folsom Lake (South Arm): *Clarksville, Pilot Hill*

Lake Natoma: *Folsom*

Slab Creek Reservoir: *Slate Mountain*

Harry L. Englebright Lake: *French Corral, Oregon House, Smartville*

Lower Yuba River: *Smartville, Browns Valley, Yuba City*

Cosumnes River Sloughs / Mokelumne River: *Galt, Bruceville*

Stanislaus River: *Knights Ferry, Oakdale*

Lake Berryessa: *Lake Berryessa, Chiles Valley, Walter Springs, Brooks, Monticello Dam*

Note: A listing of individual 7.5 min. map sheets may be ordered from USGS by requesting a *California Index to Topographic and Other Map Coverage* (1993) from Map Distribution, USGS Map Sales, Box 25286, Federal Center, Bldg. 810, Denver, CO 80225

Indexes and individual maps for the Western States region may also be purchased by contacting the USGS Public Inquiries Office in Menlo Park, California; tel: 650-329-4390; fax: 650-329-5130.

Additional USGS maps available on a smaller scale:
County Map Series, 1: 100 000 scale
30 X 60 Minute Series, 1: 100 000 scale
1 X 2 Degree series, 1: 250 000 scale

[Editor's note: The higher the map scale ratio, the smaller the detail available. One inch on a map scale of 1: 24 000 represents 2000 feet; one inch on a scale of 1:250 000 represents about 4 miles. A small-scale map = less detail; a large-scale map = greater detail. This terminology is often misunderstood.]

U. S. Forest Service Maps
El Dorado National Forest
Stanislaus National Forest
Tahoe National Forest

California State Maps

Department of Boating
and Waterways,
Department of Parks
and Recreation Maps:
A Boating Trail Guide to the North and Middle Forks of the American River.

A Boating Trail Guide to the American River Parkway, Safety Hints and Guide Map.

Miscellaneous Maps

Crystal Basin Recreation Area Map, Sacramento Municipal Utility District (SMUD), 1995

Englebright Lake Recreation Guide / Map, U.S. Army Corps of Engineers, 1993

Outdoor Recreation Guide, Northern and Southern California, U.S. Army Corps of Engineers, 1994

Stanislaus River Parks Recreation Guide / Map, U.S. Army Corps of Engineers, 1993

Commercial Map Companies

Aquamaps
P.O. Box 162961
Sacramento, CA 95816
Tel: 916-456-4137

Compass Maps Inc.
1172 Kansas Avenue
Modesto, CA 95351
Tel: 209-529-5017

De Lorme Mapping Company
P.O. Box 298
Freeport, ME 04032
Tel: 207-865-4171

Erickson Maps
337 17th Street, Suite 211
Oakland, CA 94612
Tel: 510-893-3685

Family Fun Publications
P.O. Box 21-4152
Sacramento, CA 95821
Tel: 916-481-7422
(recreation maps & guides)

FHS Maps
(Fishing Hot Spots, Inc.)
P.O. Box 1167
2389 Air Park Road
Rhinelander, WI 54501
Tel: 800-500-MAPS (6277)

Fish n Map Company, Inc.
8536 West 79th Avenue
Arvada, CO 80005
Tel: 303-421-5994;
fax: 303-420-0843

Metsker Maps
P.O. Box 110669
Tacoma, WA 98411
Tel: 253-588-5222

Maps on CD-ROM
Outdoors on Disk
1563 Solano Avenue
Berkeley, CA 94707
(Northern California topo-
graphic maps on CD-ROM)

Wildflower Productions
(TOPO! Interactive maps on
CD-ROM; 7.5 minute
USGS topographic maps)
375 Alabama Street, Suite 230
San Francisco, CA 94110
Tel: 415-558-8700;
fax: 415-558-9700
info@topo.com
website: www.topo.com

Map Sales (Sacramento Area)

California Surveying and
Drafting Supply
4733 Auburn Boulevard
Sacramento, CA 95841
Tel: 916-344-0232 / 1-800-243-1414
Fax: 916-344-2998

Ogden Surveying Equipment Co.
5520 Elvas Avenue
Sacramento, CA 95819
Tel: 916-451-7253 / 1-800-350-6277
Fax: 916-451-2865

REI (Recreational Equipment
Incorporated)
1790 Exposition Parkway
Sacramento, CA 95815
Tel: 916-924-8900

Appendix 2

Federal, State and County Agencies

U.S. Forest Service

Tahoe National Forest Head-
quarters
Hwy. 49 & Coyote Street
Nevada City, CA 95959
Tel: 916-265-4531

El Dorado National Forest
Information Cntr.
3070 Camino Heights Drive
Camino, CA 95709
Tel: 916-644-6048

Stanislaus National Forest
Forest Supervisor
19777 Greenly Road
Sonora, CA 95370
Tel: 209-532-3671

Other Federal Agencies

Army Corps of Engineers
Natural Resource Management
650 Capitol Mall
Sacramento, CA 95814
Tel: 916-551-2112

BLM
(Bureau of Land Management)
2800 Cottage Way
Room E-2841
Sacramento, CA 95825
Tel: 916-978-4574

USGS
(United States Geological Survey)
Department of the Interior
555 Battery Street, Rm. 504
San Francisco, CA 94111
Tel: 415-556-5627

USGS: Public Inquiries Office
345 Middlefield Road
Mail Stop #532
Menlo Park, CA 94025
Tel: 650-329-5130;
Fax: 650-329-5130

State Agencies

California State Office
2135 Butano Drive
Sacramento, CA
BLM / NPS / FS Recreation
Information:
Tel: 916-978-4400

California Department of
Boating and Waterways
1629 S Street
Sacramento, CA 95814
Tel: 916-445-2615

California Department
of Conservation
Division of Mines and
Geology Publications and
Information Office
801 K Street, 12th floor
MS-14-33
Sacramento, CA 95814-3532
Tel: 916-445-5716

California Department of
Fish and Game
1419 Ninth Street
Sacramento, CA 95814
Tel: 916-445-3531

California Department of Parks
and Recreation
P.O. Box 2390
Sacramento, CA 95811
Tel: 916-445-4624 / 800-444-7275

California Department of
Transportation (CALTRANS)
1120 N street
Sacramento, CA 95814
Tel (local): 916-445-7623
Tel (outside local calling area):
800-427-7623
Tel (maps): 916-654-3206

State Parks General Information
Tel: 916-653-6995
Reservation phone number
(new as of 01/98)
1-800-444-PARK
(between 8:00 a.m. and 5 p.m.,
seven days a week)

State Districts
(American River area)

Auburn State Recreation Area
Tel: 916-885-4527

Folsom Lake State Recreation
Area (Flsm)
Tel: 916-988-0205

Folsom Lake Marina
Tel: 916-933-1300

County Agencies

El Dorado County Parks &
Recreation
2850 Fair Lane Court
Placerville, CA 95667
Tel: 916-621-5353;
fax: 916-621-7433

Sacramento County Regional
Department of Parks
& Recreation
4040 Bradshaw Road
Sacramento, CA 95827
Tel: 916-366-2072

City Agencies

Folsom City Parks & Recreation
Tel: 916-355-7285

Sacramento City Parks &
Recreation
General Information
Tel: 916-277-6060

Appendix 3

Organizations, Clubs & Special Programs

American Canoe Association
(ACA)
7432 Alban Station Boulevard,
Suite B-226
Springfield, VA 22150-2311
Tel: 703-451-0141
e-mail: ACADirect@aol.com
website: www.aca-paddler.org

American Red Cross
(Sacramento Area Chapter)
P.O. Box 160167
8928 Volunteer Lane
Sacramento, CA 95826-3221
Tel: 916-368-3167;
fax: 916-985-7312

American River Conservancy
8913 Highway 49
P.O. Box 562
Coloma, CA 95613
Tel: 916-621-1224

American River Parkway
Foundation
P.O. Box 276566
Sacramento, CA 95827
Tel: 916-456-7423

American White Water
Affiliation (AWA)
P.O. Box 636
Margaretville, NY 12455
Tel: 914-586-2355;
fax: 301-589-6121
e-mail: awa@compuserve.com
website: www.awa.org/

California Floater's Society
Mill Valley, CA
Tel: 415-435-7936

California State University
Sacramento
Aquatic and Boat Safety Center
1901 Hazel Avenue
Rancho Cordova, CA 95670
Tel: 916-985-7239;
fax: 916-985-7312

Cosumnes River Preserve
The Nature Conservancy
6500 Desmond Drive
Galt, CA 95632
Tel: 916-491-1820

Environmental Traveling
Companions (etc)
*(wilderness adventures for disabled
& disadvantaged people; school
groups, corporate groups, etc.)*
Fort Mason Center, Bldg. C
San Francisco, CA 94123
Tel: 415-474-7662;
fax: 415-474-3919

Friends of the River
128 J Street, Second Floor
Sacramento, CA 95814
Tel: 916-442-3155

Gold Country Paddlers
(whitewater club)
Sacramento Region:
Rick Parnell
530-333-1999

San Francisco Bay Area:
Elaine Baden
510-582-2860

Hui-O-Hawaii of Sacramento
(outrigger racing & paddling
club)
Bob & Marilyn Steele
Tel: 916-988-2419

Nevada County Paddlers
Unlimited
Nevada City, CA
Tel: 916-265-3780

River City Paddlers
(racing club)
c/o Nancy Carroll, Treasurer
125 Casselman Street
Folsom, CA 95630
Tel: 916-362-2804

Sierra Club River Touring
Section (RTS)
c/o Bill Cutts
30,000-256 Kasson Rd.
Tracy, CA 95376

Sierra Club Singles
(Mother Lode Chapter)
1500 West El Camino,
Suite 13, #102
Sacramento, CA 95833
Tel: 916-557-4114
innercite.com/~singles/

Stone Lakes National
Wildlife Refuge
Office: 2233 Watt Avenue,
Suite 375
Sacramento, CA 95825-0509
Tel: 916-979-2085
Location: Elk Grove, CA

Appendix 4
Training, Outfitting & Rentals

Paddling Schools

American Red Cross
(Sacramento Area Chapter)
Tel: 916-368-3167;
fax: 916-368-3224

California Canoe & Kayak
Tel: 800-366-9804;
fax: 916-631-1424

CSUS Aquatic and
Boat Safety Center
Tel: 16-985-7239;
fax: 916-985-7312

Current Adventures
Tel: 916-642-9755

South Fork Custom
Canoe Outfitting
Tel: 916-853-8565

Outfitting & Rentals

Adventure Sports
6040 Fair oaks Boulevard
Carmichael, CA 95608
Tel: 916-971-1800

California Canoe & Kayak
Nimbus Winery, Sacramento
12401 Folsom Boulevard, Suite 205
Rancho Cordova, CA 95742
Tel: 916-353-1880
e-mail: calkayak@aol.com
website: www.calkayak.com

CSUS Aquatic and
Boat Safety Center
(rentals on Lake Natoma only)
1901 Hazel Avenue
Rancho Cordova, CA 95670
Tel: 916-985-7239;
fax: 916-985-7312

Klepper West
Western Folding Kayak Center
6155 Mt. Aukum Road
Somerset, CA 95684-0130
Tel: 530-626-8647

South Fork Custom
Canoe Outfitting
2933 Gold Pan Court, Suite A
Rancho Cordova, CA 95670
Tel: 916-853-8565
(proof of canoe proficiency
prior to MOVING WATER
rentals)

West Marine
(for boat accessories)
9500 Micron Avenue
Sacramento, CA 95827
Tel: 916-366-3300;
fax: 916-366-8872

Wilderness Sports
11335 Folsom Boulevard
Rancho Cordova, CA
Tel: 916-985-3555
website:
www.wildernesssports.com

Appendix 5

Paddle Sports Magazines

American White Water
Journal of the American White
Water Affiliation
(bi-monthly)
P.O. Box 636
Margaretville, NY 12544

Canoe Journal
(published by *Canoe & Kayak*)
P.O. Box 3146
Kirkland, WA 98083
Tel: 425-827-6363/
fax: 425-827-1893
website: www.canoekayak.com

Canoe & Kayak
(bi-monthly)
P.O. Box 3146
Kirkland, WA 98083-3146
Tel: 425-827-6363;
fax: 425-827-1893
e-mail: c&k@canoekayak.com
website: www.canoekayak.com
(*Note:* The magazine publishes a
yearly Buyer's Guide every
December issue.)

Kayak Touring
(published by *Canoe & Kayak*)
P.O. Box 3146
Kirkland, WA 98083-3146
Tel: 425-827-6363;
fax: 425-827-1893

Northern California Trails
(bi-monthly)
P.O. Box 5048
Chico, CA 95927
Tel/fax: 916-898-1032

Paddler Magazine
(bi-monthly)
7432 Alban Station, Suite B-226
Springfield, VA 22150
Tel: 703-455-3419;
fax: 703-451-2245
(*Note:* Magazine publishes a
yearly buyer's directory every
December issue.)

Sierra Heritage Magazine
P.O. Box 9148
Auburn, CA 95604
Tel: 916-823-3986

Sea Kayaker
(bi-monthly)
P.O. Box 17170
Seattle, WA 98107-9948
Tel: 206-789-9536;
fax: 206-781-1141
e-mail:
mail@seakayakermag.com
website:
www.seakayakermag.com

WoodenBoat
(bi-monthly)
P.O. Box 54766
Boulder, CO 80322-4766
1-800-877-5284

Bibliography & References

Please Note: Telephone numbers, fax numbers and, in some cases, addresses have been included for references that may prove difficult to access. Abbreviations are defined as follows:*n.d.* (no publication date available); *n.p.* (no publication information could be found).

GENERAL

Abbey, Edward. *A Voice Crying in the Wilderness (Vox Clamantis in Deserto) Notes From A Secret Journal.* New York: St. Martin's Press, 1989.

Aiken, Zora and David. *Simple Tent Camping: Basics of Camping from Car or Canoe.* Camden, ME: Ragged Mountain Press, n.d.

American Canoe Association. *Introduction to Paddling: Canoeing Basics for Lakes and Rivers.* Birmingham, AL: Menasha Ridge Press, 1996.

Backes, David. *The Wilderness Companion: Reflections for the Back-Country Traveler.* Minocqua, WI: Nortwood Press, Inc., 1992.

Bechdel, Les and Slim Ray. *River Rescue: A Manual for Whitewater Safety*, 3rd ed. Boston: Appalachian Mountain Club Books, 1997.

Burch, David. *Fundamentals of Kayak Navigation,* 2nd ed. Old Saybrook, CT: The Globe Pequot Press, 1993.

Cassidy, Jim, Bill Cross and Fryar Calhoun. *Western Whitewater from the Rockies to the Pacific.* Berkeley: North Fork Press, 1994.

Cassidy, John. *The Klutz Book of Knots.* Palo Alto, CA: Klutz Press, 1985.

Caughey, John & Laree, eds. *California Heritage: An Anthology of History and Literature.* Los Angeles: Ward Ritchie Press, 1964, 2nd printing.

Cunningham, Richard W. *California Indian Watercraft.* San Luis Obispo: EZ Nature Books, 1989.

Daniel, Linda. *Kayak Cookery: A Handbook of Provisions and Recipes.* Chester, CT: Globe Pequot Press, 1986.

Department of Conservation. *California Geology.* Division of Mines and Geology, Sacramento: (published bi-monthly).
[tel: 916-445-5716; fax: 916-327-1853]

Dyson, George. *Baidarka The Kayak.* Seattle: Alaska Northwest Books, 1997, 5th printing.

Getchell, Annie. *The Essential Outdoor Gear Manual: Equipment Care & Repair for Outdoors People.* Camden, ME: Ragged Mountain Press, 1995.
[1-800-822-8158]

Guillion, Laurie. *Canoeing and Kayaking Instruction Manual.* Birmingham: Menasha Ridge Press, 1987.

Hansen, David & Judy. *Canoe Tripping with Children: Unique Advice for Keeping Children Comfortable.* Merrillville, IN: ICS Books, 1990. [1-800-541-7323]

Harris, Thomas. *Down the Wild Rivers: A Guide to the Streams of California.* San Francisco: Chronicle Books, 1972.

Hill, Mary. *Geology of the Sierra Nevada.* Berkeley: University of California Press, 1975.

———. *California Landscapes: Origin And Evolution.* Berkeley: University of California Press, 1984.

Howard, Arthur D. *Geologic History of Middle California.* Berkeley: University of California Press, 1979.

Jacobson, Cliff. *Canoeing Wild Rivers: A Primer to North American Expedition Canoeing.* Merrillville, IN: ICS Books Inc., 1984.

———. *Canoeing and Camping Beyond the Basics.* Merrillville: ICS Books Inc., 1992.

———. *The Basic Essentials of Canoeing.* Merrillville: ICS Books Inc., 1995, 7th printing.

———. *The Basic Essentials of Map and Compass.* Merrillville: ICS Books Inc., n. d.

Logue, Victoria and Frank with Mark Carroll. *Kids Outdoors: Skills and Knowledge for Outdoor Adventure.* Camden, ME: Ragged Mountain Press, n. d.

Mason, Bill. *Song of the Paddle, An Illustrated Guide to Wilderness Camping.* Minocqua, WI: Northwood Press, 1988. [1-800-336-5666]

McConnell, Mary M. *Outdoor Adventures with Kids.* Dallas: Taylor Publishing Company, 1996.

McKinnon-McDade, Stephanie. "Call of the Wild." *Sacramento Bee,* Sunday, November 23, 1997, Travel Section: T1. (Women in the Wild program)

Mckown, Doug. *Canoeing Safety & Rescue: A Handbook of Safety and Rescue Procedures for Lake and River Canoeists.* Calgary: Rocky Mountain Books, n.d.

McPhee, John. *Survival of the Bark Canoe.* New York: Warner Books edition, published by Farrar, Straus and Giroux, Inc., 1975.

Mills, Sheila. *The Outdoor Dutch Oven Cookbook.* Camden, ME: Ragged Mountain Press, 1997.

Moore, Patrick. *Exploring the Night Sky with Binoculars,* 3rd ed. Cambridge: Cambridge University Press, 1997

Olsen, Sigurd F. *The Lonely Land.* New York: Alfred A. Knopf, Inc., 1961.

———*Sigurd F. Olson's Wilderness Days.* New York: Alfred A. Knopf, Inc., 1972.

Palmer, Steve. *Stanislaus: The Struggle for a River.* Berkeley: University of California Press, 1982.

Ray, Slim. *The Canoe Handbook: Techniques for Mastering the Sport of Canoeing.* Harrisburg, PA: Stackpole Books, 1992. [1-800-READ-NOW]

Ross, Cindy and Todd Gladfelter. *Kids in the Wild.* Seattle: The Mountaineers Press, 1995.

Schwind, Dick. *West Coast River Touring: Rogue River Canyon and South.* Beaverton, OR: Touchstone Press, 1974.

Seidman, David. *The Essential Sea Kayaker: A Complete Course for the Open-Water Paddler.* Camden, ME: Ragged Mountain Press, 1992.

Snyder, Gary. *Mountains and Rivers Without End.* Washington D.C.: Counterpoint, 1996. [P.O. Box 65793, Washington DC 20035-5793]

State of California, Department of Parks & Recreation, Department of Navigation & Ocean Development. *Boating Trails For California Rivers: An Element of the California Recreational Trails Plan.* Sacramento: SPO, May 1978.

Stienstra, Tom. *California Fishing: The Complete Guide.* San Francisco: Foghorn Press, 1995–96 edition.

Wright, Terry. *Guide to Geology and Rapids, South Fork American River.* Forestville, CA: Wilderness Interpretation Publications, 1981. n.p. [P.O. Box 279-P, Forestville, CA 95436]

Teale, Edwin Way, ed. *The Wilderness World of John Muir.* Boston: Houghton Mifflin Company, 1954.

Tilton, Buck and Frank Hubbell. *Medicine in the Back Country.* Merrillville, IN: ICS Books Inc., 1990.

Walbridge, Charlie. *Knots for Paddlers.* Birmingham: Menasha Ridge Press, 1995.

Wilderness Conservancy. *The American River: North, Middle, & South Forks.* Auburn, CA: Protect American River Canyons, 1989. [PARC, Box 9312, 95604]

Wilkerson, James A. M. D. *Medicine for Mountaineering & Other Wilderness Activities.* Seattle: The Mountaineers, 1992, 4th ed.

Wyatt, Mike. *The Basic Essentials of Sea Kayaking.* Merrillville, IN: ICS Books Inc., 1996, 2nd ed.

Yogi, Stan, ed. *Highway 99: A Literary Journey through California's Great Central Valley.* Berkeley, CA: Heyday Books in conjunction with California Council for the Humanities, 1996.

GEOGRAPHIC AREAS

The American River, Lake Valley Reservoir, Lake Clementine, Slab Creek, Folsom Lake & Lake Natoma

Dirksen, Greg and Renee Reeves. *Recreation Lakes of California, Tenth Edition.* Burbank: Recreation Sales Publishing, 1993. [310-474-8045]

Dwyer, Ann. *Canoeing Waters of California.* Kentfield, CA: GBH Press, 1973.

Fair Oaks Historical Society. *Fair Oaks . . . The Early Years.* Fair Oaks, CA: 1995.

5 Easy Paddles: California 2. Elkhorn Slough, American River, Merced River, Newport Bay, Navarro River. 60 min. Placid Videos, 1994. [800-549-0046]

Jeneid, Michael. *Adventure Kayaking: Trips from the Russian River to Monterey.* Berkeley: Wilderness Press, 1998.

McDonnell, Lawrence R., Ed. *Rivers of California.* San Francisco: Pacific Gas & Electric Company, 1962.

Palmer, Steve. *America by Rivers.* Washington D.C: Island Press, 1996.

Sanborn, Margaret. *The American River of El Dorado*, Rivers of America Series. New York: Holt, Rinehart & Winston, 1974.

Stienstra, Tom. *California Boating and Water Sports.* San Francisco: Foghorn Press, 1996.

Thomas, Bill. *American Rivers, A Natural History.* New York: W.W. Norton, 1978.

White, Jim L. "A River I Remember," *Sierra Heritage Magazine*, May / June 1991. 60–63.

Wilderness Conservancy. *The American River North, Middle, & South Forks.* Auburn, CA: Protect American River Canyons, 1989.

Wright, Terry. *Guide to Geology and Rapids, South Fork American River.* Forestville, CA: Wilderness Interpretation Publications, 1981. n.p.

Lower Stanislaus River

Dwyer, Ann. *Canoeing Waters of California.* Kentfield, CA: GBH Press, 1973.

Harris, Thomas. *Down the Wild Rivers: A Guide to the Streams of California.* San Francisco: Chronicle Books, 1972.

McDonnell, Lawrence R., ed. *Rivers of California.* San Francisco: Pacific Gas & Electric Company, 1962.

Palmer, Steve. *Stanislaus: The Struggle for a River.* Berkeley: University of California Press, 1982.

Stienstra, Tom. *California Boating and Water Sports.* San Francisco: Foghorn Press, 1996.

———. *California Fishing—The Complete Guide.* San Francisco: Foghorn Press, 1995–96 edition.

Mokelumne / Cosumnes River Confluence & Back Sloughs

Dillon, Richard and Steve Simmons, photographer. *Delta Country.* Novato, CA: Presidio Press, 1982.

Harris, Thomas. *Down the Wild Rivers, A Guide to the Streams of California.* San Francisco: Chronicle Books, 1972.

McDonnell, Lawrence R., ed. *Rivers of California.* San Francisco: Pacific Gas & Electric Company, 1962.

Dirksen, Greg and Renee Reeves. *Recreation Lakes of California, Tenth Edition.* Burbank, CA: Recreation Sales Publishing, 1993.

Dwyer, Ann. *Canoeing Waters of California.* Kentfield, CA: GBH Press, 1973.

McDonnell, Lawrence R., ed. *Rivers of California.* San Francisco: Pacific Gas & Electric Company, 1962.

Stienstra, Tom. *California Boating and Water Sports.* San Francisco: Foghorn Press, 1996.

———. *California Fishing—The Complete Guide.* San Francisco: Foghorn Press, 1995–96 ed.

Lake Berryessa

Dirksen, Greg and Renee Reeves. *Recreational Lakes of California, Tenth Edition.* Burbank, CA: Recreational Sales Publishing, Inc., 1993.

Stienstra, Tom. *California Boating and Water Sports.* San Francisco: Foghorn Press, 1996.

———. *California Fishing The Complete Guide.* San Francisco: Foghorn Press, 1995–96 edition.

RELATED SUBJECTS

Geology:

Alt, David D. and Donald W. Hyndman. *Roadside Geology of Northern California.* Missoula: Mountain Press, 1978.

Bailey, Edgar H., ed. *Geology of Northern California.* San Francisco: California Division of Mines and Geology, Bulletin 190, 1966.

Clark, William B., ed. *Gold Districts of California.* San Francisco: California Division of Mines and Geology, Bulletin 139, 1970.

Cox, Dan. "Rocks & Rivers: A Primer on River Geology." *River Runner,* October 1990. 22–27.

Cox, John D. "River tour: A rocky slice through geological time," *Sacramento Bee.* May 15,1995, Discovery Section, front page.

Department of Conservation. *California Geology.* Division of Mines and Geology, Sacramento (bi-monthly). [tel: 916-445-5716; fax: 916-327-1853]

Hill, Mary. *Geology of the Sierra Nevada.* Berkeley: University of California Press, 1975.

———. *California Landscapes: Origin And Evolution.* Berkeley: University of California Press, 1984.

Howard, Arthur D. *Geologic History of Middle California.* Berkeley: University of California Press, 1979.

McPhee, John. *Assembling California.* New York: Farrar, Straus and Giroux, 1993.

Morrison, Paul D. *Placer Gold Deposits of the Sierra Nevada.* Baldwin Park, CA: Gem Guides Book Company, 1997.

Natural and Human History:

Aginsky, Burt W. and Ethel G. *Deep Valley: The Pomo Indians of California.* New York: Stein and Day, 1971.

Bakker, Elna. *An Island Called California—An Ecological Introduction to its Natural Communities.* Berkeley: University of California Press, 1971.

Browning, Peter. *Place Names of the Sierra Nevada from Abbot to Zumwalt.* Berkeley: Wilderness Press, 1986.

California State Department of Education. *The Central Valley Project.* Sacramento, 1942.

Farquhar, Francis P. *History of the Sierra Nevada.* Berkeley: University of California Press, 1969 edition.

Fradkin, Philip L. *The Seven States of California: Human and Natural History.* New York: Henry Holt and Company, 1995.

Gudde, Erwin G. *California Gold Camps.* Berkeley: University of California Press, 1975.

Heizer, Robert F. and Albert B. Elsasser. *The Natural World of the California Indians.* Berkeley: University of California Press, 1980.

Hill, Russell B. *California Mountain Ranges; The California Geographic Series.* Billings, MT: Falcon Press, 1986.

Hinkle, George and Bliss, edited by Milo M. Quaife. *Sierra-Nevada Lakes; The American Lakes Series.* Indianapolis & New York: Bobbs-Merrill Company, 1949.

Holden, William M. *Sacramento Excursions into Its History and Natural World.* Fair Oaks, CA: Two Rivers Publishing, 1987.

Hoover, Mildred B., Hero Eugene Rensch, and Ethel Grace Rensch. *Historic Spots in California.* 1962 ed. Revised Douglas E. Kyle. Stanford: Stanford University Press, 1995.

Johnson, Stephen, Gerald W. Haslam, and Robert Dawson. *The Great Central Valley: California's Heartland.* Berkeley: University of California Press in association with the California Academy of Sciences, 1993.

Johnston, Verna R. *California Forests and Woodlands: A Natural History.* Berkeley: University of California Press, 1994.

Lee, W. Storrs. *The Sierra.* New York: G. P. Putnam, 1962.

Lewis, Oscar. *High Sierra Country.* Reno & Las Vegas: University of Nevada Press, 1955.

Margolin, Malcolm, ed. *The Way We Lived: California Indian Reminiscences, Stories and Songs.* Berkeley: Heyday Books, 1981.

Mc Millon, Bill. *Seasonal Guide to the Natural Year, Northern California; Month by Month Guide to Natural Events.* Golden, CO: Fulcrum Publishing, 1995.

Schoenherr, Allen A. *A Natural History of California.* Berkeley: University of California Press, 1995.

Smith, Jo, ed. *The Outdoor World of the Sacramento Region: A Local Field Guide.* Sacramento. (Originally *Natural History Guide for the Sacramento Region,* Effie Yeaw, 1963). American River Natural History Association in cooperation with Sacramento County Office of Education, 1993.

Storer, Tracy I. and Robert L. Usinger. *Sierra Nevada Natural History,* 13th ed. Berkeley: University of California Press, 1963.

Wiegand, Steve. "Gold Rush Sesquicentennial." *Sacramento Bee,* Sunday, 18 January 1998, A1. (A special four-part edition.)

Whitney, Stephen. *The Sierra Nevada,* 6th ed. San Francisco, CA: Sierra Club Books, 1979.

Plants, Animals & Insects

Balls, Edward K. *Early Uses of California Plants.* Berkeley: University of California Press, 1962.

Brown, Philip R. *A Field Guide to Snakes of California.* Houston: Gulf Publishing Co., 1997.

Brown, Vinson, Henry Weston Jr., and Jerry Buzzell. *Handbook of California Birds.* 3rd ed., Happy Camp, CA: Naturegraph Publishers, 1986.

Cockrum, Lendell E. and Yar Petryszyn. *Mammals of California and Nevada.* Tucson: Treasure Chest Publications, 1994.

Cogswell, Howard L. *Water Birds of California.* Berkeley: University of California Press, 1977.

Crittenden, Mabel. *Trees of the West.* Millbrae, CA: Celestial Arts, 1977.

Crittenden, Mabel and Dorothy Telfer. *Wildflowers of the West.* Millbrae, CA: Celestial Arts, 1975.

Dalrymple, Byron. *Sportman's Guide to Game Fish.* New York: World Publishing Co., 1968.

Garth, John S. and J.W. Tilden. *California Butterflies.* Berkeley: University of California Press, 1986.

Head, W. S. *The California Chaparral: An Elfin Forest.* Happy Camp, CA: Naturegraph Publishers.

Howe, William H. *The Butterflies of North America.* Garden City, NY: Doubleday & Company, 1975.

Mallette, Robert D. and Gordon I. Gould Jr. *Raptors of California.* Sacramento: California Department of Fish and Game, 1976.

Munz, Phillip A. *California Spring Wild Flowers: From the Base of the Sierra Nevada and Southern Mountains to the Sea.* Berkeley: University of California Press, 1961.

Ornduff, Robert. *Introduction to California Plant Life.* Berkeley: University of California Press, 1986.

Orr, Robert T. and Dorthy B. Orr. *Mushrooms of Western North America.* Berkeley: University of California Press, 1979.

Pavlik, Bruce M., Pamela C. Muick, Sharon G. Johnson, and Marjorie Popper. *Oaks of California.* Los Olivos, CA: Cachuma Press, 1995.

Peattie, Donald Cukross. *A Natural History of Western Trees.* Boston: Houghton Mifflin, 1981.

Peterson, Roger T. *A Field Guide To Western Birds,* 2nd ed. Boston: Houghton Mifflin, 1961.

Pickett, Edwin R. *Birds of Central California,* 2nd printing. Sacramento, CA: reprinted from the *Sacramento Bee Daily Newspaper,* 1972.

Powell, Jerry A. and Charles L. Hogue. *California Insects.* Berkeley: University of California Press, 1979.

Sacramento Department of Parks and Recreation. *Fishing in Sacramento County.* Sacramento: County of Sacramento, 1983.

Schmidt, Marjorie G. *Growing California Native Plants.* Berkeley: University of California Press, 1980.

Spellenberg, Richard. *The Audubon Society Field Guide to North American Wildflowers; Western Region.* New York: Alfred A. Knopf, 1979.

Paddling Basics & Tips

Apt, Scott. "A Case of Weight" (Lifting and Carrying Your Kayak). *Sea Kayaker,* August, 1997. 16-17.

Bennett, Jeff and Tonya. "Draw & Shoot." *Canoe & Kayak,* December, 1996. 37. (How to obtain permits; addresses, etc.)

Chitwood, Bryan, "Increasingly Sophisticated, Dry Bags Come of Age." *Canoe & Kayak,* March 1998, 72–76.

Cox, Dan. "Mechanics of Rapids." *River Runner,* June 1989. n.p.

From Here To There: Canoe Basics, videocassette 68 min. Joe Holt Productions, 1997.

Gabbard, Andrea. "17 Water Shoes and Sandals." *Canoe & Kayak,* May, 1997. 132–135.

Gronseth, George. "Avoiding Double Trouble." *Sea Kayaker,* February, 1997: 59–60.

Gullion, Laurie. "Canoeing: Tandem Talk." *Canoe & Kayak,* December, 1996, 14. (How partners communicate.)

Hanson, Jonathan. "Packing for Performance." *Sea Kayaker,* February 1996, 33–35.

———. "Extra Cush For Your Tush," *Sea Kayaker,* August 1997, 57–59.

Jacobson, Cliff. "Get the Bugs Out of Your Canoe Trips," *Canoe & Kayak,* March, 1998, 17.

———. "Custom Touches for Your Canoe." *Paddler,* October 1997, 80–83.

Kayak Touring. "Finding Your Way Along the Waterways." 1995. 68.

———. " Predicting Your Weather." 1995, 67.

———. "The Back Azimuth as a Piloting Tool." 1995, 70.

Kesselheim, Alan S. "Outfitting Family Trips." *Canoe & Kayak*, May 1997, 52–57.

Knapp, Andy. "Topping A Car Solo." *Sea Kayaker*, October 1996, 12. (How to load your boat on top of your vehicle by yourself.)

———. "Long-Haul Packing." *Canoe & Kayak*, August 1996, 10.

———. "Tune Up Your Kayak for the New Season." *Canoe & Kayak*, March 1998, 21.

Kress, Debbie. "The Trials and Tribulations of Paddling Double." *Sea Kayaker*, February 1997, 56–58.

Lessels, Bruce. "Material Matters." *Canoe & Kayak*, March 1997, 44-48. (Canoe & kayak construction techniques and materials.)

McCormack, Edward. "Preventing Mildew Damage." *Sea Kayaker*, August 1996, 60.

Meyer, John. "Ruler of the Seas: Dealing with the Effects of Wind and Waves." *Canoe & Kayak*, March 1998, 24.

Path of the Paddle: Quiet Water, videocassette 54 min. Northword Press, Inc., 1977.

Performance Sea Kayaking: "The Basics. . . and Beyond," videocassette 58 min. Kent Ford and John C. Davis. Performance Video and Instruction Inc, Durango, CO.

Rasmussen, Ken. "Custom Outfitting with Foam." *Sea Kayaker*, February, 1998, 42–47.

Richardson-Korleski, Lori and Janet Fullwood. "Camp Cookin." *Sacramento Bee*, Wednesday, August 6,1997, Section F, p. F1.

Schumann, Roger. "In Search of the Perfect Sea Kayaking Shoes." *Sea Kayaker*, October 1997, 20–25.

Sea Kayaking: "Getting Started," videocassette, 84 min. Larry Holman and Jack Lyons, Moving Pictures, 1995.

Surf Kayaking Fundamentals, videocassete 20 min. Lull Productions, 1995. (Basic skills necessary for all aspects of kayak surfing.)

Navigation

Be Your Own Map Expert. Reviewed in AlpenBooks Catalog (January-February 1997), 112. (For kids: making and reading maps.)

Beier, Udo and Scott Cunningham. "Navigation by Satellite." *Sea Kayaker*, Fall 1993, 40–43.

GPS. Videocassette #N3883. Los Angeles: Bennett Marine Video. [tel: 213-951-7570; fax: 213-951-7595]

"GPS Global Positioning Systems." *Canoe & Kayak.* Dec. 1994, 32.

Harrison, David F., "The Orienteering Compass for the Navigator." *Canoe & Kayak,* July 1994, 21.

Jacobson, Cliff. *"The Basic Essentials of Map and Compass."* Merrillville, IN: ICS Books Inc., n.d. 48pp.

Letham, Lawrence. *GPS Made: Easy Using Global Positioning System in the Outdoors.* Seattle: The Mountaineers, 1995.

Map Scales, U. S. Department of the Interior. [Geological Survey National Cartographic Information Center (NCIC). Reston-ESIC, 507 National Cntr., Reston, VA 22092. Tel: 703-860-6045]

————. *Finding Your Way with Map and Compass.*

Nevin, Bradley. "Which Way No More." *Kayak Touring,* 1995, 34.

Redmond, Kevin & Dan Murphy. "Global Positioning Systems." *Canoe & Kayak,* March, 1997, 90-96.

REI Product Information Guide. "GPS Receivers," Fall 1997, (1pg.).

————."Compasses," Aug. 1993.

Seidman, David. *The Essential Wilderness Navigator.* Camden, ME: Ragged Mountain Press, n.d.

"Using the UTM System" (Universal Transverse Mercator grid system), *Canoe & Kayak,* December 1994, 23.

Guides and Catalogs

Blake, Tupper Ansel and Peter Steinhart. *Tracks in the Sky. Wildlife and Wetlands of the Pacific Flyway.* San Francisco: Chronicle Books in association with the National Audubon Society, 1987.

Beginner's Guide to Canoeing and Kayaking. Kirkland, Washington: Canoe & Kayak Magazine.

Burgess, Evan, *South Fork of the American River Watershed Guide,* American Land Conservancy, n.d. 1pg. (California Canoe & Kayak Store, Oakland, CA.)

California State Parks. *Reserved Camping in California State Parks.* Sacramento: GPO, January 1995.

Dalrymple, Byron. *Sportman's Guide to Game Fish.* New York: The World Publishing Co., 1968.

Hillinger, Charles. *Hillinger's California.* Santa Barbara: Capra Press, 1997.

Kellogg, Zip, ed. *The Whole Paddler's Catalog*. Camden, ME: Ragged Mountain Press, 1996.

Olmsted, Gerald W. *The Best of the Sierra Nevada*. New York: Crown Publishers, 1991.

Preston,Thomas and Elizabeth. *The Double Eagle Guide to Western State Parks: Volume III, Far West: California / Nevada.* Billings, MT: Discovery Publishing, 1991.

REI (Recreational Equipment Incorporated)
Product Information Guides:
Binoculars, Fall 1997.
Canoe Camping Gear List, February 1995.
Canoes, Spring 1997.
Canoe Paddles, Spring 1997.
Compasses, August 1993.
GPS Receivers, Fall 1997.
Kayak Paddles, Spring 1997
Kayaks, Spring 1997.

Riviere, Bill. *The L. L. Bean Guide to the Outdoors*. New York: Random House, 1981.

Shears, Nick and David Shears. *Paddle America: A Guide to Trips & Outfitters in All 50 States.* Washington D.C.: Starfish Press, 1996.

Stratton, George. *Recreation Guide to California National Forests.* Billings, MT: Falcon Press, 1991.

Weir, Kim. *Northern California Handbook,* 2nd ed. Chico, CA: Moon Publications, Inc., 1994.